I0138981

From Empire to Republic

Hacer Bahar

From Empire to Republic

**The Role of American Missionaries in US-Ottoman
Empire Relations and their Educational Legacy**

PETER LANG

Bibliographic Information published by the Deutsche Nationalbibliothek
The Deutsche Nationalbibliothek lists this publication in the Deutsche
Nationalbibliografie; detailed bibliographic data is available online at
http://dnb.d-nb.de.

Library of Congress Cataloging-in-Publication Data
A CIP catalog record for this book has been applied for at the Library of Congress.

ISBN 978-3-631-78670-3 (Print)
E-ISBN 978-3-631-78837-0 (E-PDF)
E-ISBN 978-3-631-78838-7 (EPUB)
E-ISBN 978-3-631-78839-4 (MOBI)
DOI 10.3726/b15562

© Peter Lang GmbH
Internationaler Verlag der Wissenschaften
Berlin 2019
All rights reserved.

Peter Lang – Berlin · Bern · Bruxelles · New York · Oxford · Warszawa · Wien

All parts of this publication are protected by copyright. Any
utilisation outside the strict limits of the copyright law, without
the permission of the publisher, is forbidden and liable to
prosecution. This applies in particular to reproductions,
translations, microfilming, and storage and processing in
electronic retrieval systems.

This publication has been peer reviewed.

www.peterlang.com

Abstract

This book focuses on American missionary activities in the Ottoman Empire. After the construction of the American Board of Commissioners for Foreign Mission in 1810, American missionaries started to spread the Gospel around the world. The Ottoman Empire was perceived as a strategic place since it occupied Jerusalem. After their arrival to the empire, American Missionaries realized that proselytizing Christians of Eastern Churches and Jews is not practical. In the case of Muslims, the laws in the country did not allow people to convert. This book argues that American missionary schools are one of the best institutions that spread Western ideals. By the time they arrived to the Empire, American missionaries found a weak central authority. Some of the Ottoman officials considered that Westernization of the public institutions in the Empire can strengthen central authority. In order to protect its integrity, Ottoman Empire started to grant freedoms to the minorities. After gaining liberties, American Missionaries further strengthen their position in the Empire. This book analyzes strong image of American missionary schools through Robert College which was constructed in 1863. Robert College which reflects American ideals, preserves its distinguished place to this day.

Table of Contents

Acknowledgements

The origins of this work lie within my search for a possible research topic in American-Turkish relations that I could develop into my master's thesis. I wanted to analyse the relationship from a historical perspective, thus my research started with US-Ottoman Empire encounters. As I progressed, I realized that American missionaries played a significant role in the development of American-Ottoman diplomatic relations. Hence, I broadened my scope to include American missionaries. Furthermore, by bringing history and religious studies together, my thesis would fit the interdisciplinary approach that is taken at the Heidelberg Center for American Studies. Later the book that I received from my friend Patricia Temiz called *Fifty Years In Constantinople And Recollections of Robert College* by George Washburn gave me the idea of analyzing American missionaries within the context of their schools, thus also adding education to the subject areas under consideration. Robert College is one of the most long-standing products of American missionary activity that still continues to admit students. Robert College is also significant as it was the first American higher education institution to be established outside of the United States. The methodology of the thesis is desk research undertaken in the American Research Institute in Istanbul and at the Bosphorus and Bilkent University libraries. The thesis includes primary sources such as memoirs, letters, annual reports, catalogues, newspapers as well as secondary sources including academic journals, books and Master's and PhD theses. Apart from archival research, the thesis also retrieved the primary sources via secondary sources due to limited access online. Primary sources played a strong role in this thesis as they provided figures, dates and depicted the conditions of American missionaries in the Ottoman Empire and later Turkish Republic.

This work is the result of my MA thesis and there are many institutions and individuals to thank. At the top of my list of acknowledgments must be Heidelberg Center for American Studies which offered me an academic home and intellectual encouragement and enabled me to realise my academic aims that I had formulated when I was an undergraduate at the University of Bilkent. Special thanks are due to the Leonie Wild Foundation whose financial support immensely assisted me during my graduate studies in Heidelberg. I would like to thank the archival staff at the American Research Institute in Turkey whose help enabled me to gain access to numerous works in my research area. I must also thank my friends and family, whose support encouraged me to continue on this journey. I am grateful to Prof. Dr. Dr. h.c. Detlef Junker and Dr. Anne Sommer who guided me throughout my graduate studies. I am indebted to my supervisor, Prof. Dr. Jan Stievermann, who agreed to take on this challenge and guide the development of my work. The advice and kind words also provided by Dr. Anja Schüler, who became my second reader in this project, were invaluable. I would like to specifically thank Patricia Temiz for her insight and proofreading, and the encouragement which helped me to complete this thesis. I also would like to thank the faculty of American Culture and Literature at Bilkent University: Prof. Dr. Lale Demirtürk, Dr. Edward Kohn, Dr. Jennifer Reimer, Dr. Dennis Bryson, Dr. Daniel Johnson whose teaching during my undergraduate studies in Ankara contributed to my academic aspirations.

Introduction

Soon after the formation of the American Board of Commissioners of For-eign Missions (ABCFM) in 1810, Protestant American missionaries started to establish missions around the globe to spread the gospel. One of the most significant places missionaries aimed at settling was Jerusalem which then lay within the boundaries of the Ottoman Empire. At that time, when the first American missionaries arrived in the Ottoman Empire, it was los-ing its central power due to wars and invasions. By the late eighteenth century, with the treaty signed with Russia and Napoleon's invasion of Egypt, the Ottoman Empire further lost its power. In 1829, Greece gained independence from the Ottoman Empire with the support of the Great Powers. The rivalry between Russia and Britain with regard to expansion-ism also showed its influence in the Ottoman Empire. The Russians sought access to warm water ports, via the strategic Bosphorus Strait, and also coveted Ottoman territories in the Balkans. As the Balkan nations started to gain independence, the "Eastern Question" emerged and the Ottoman Empire became vulnerable to European incursions. In order to regain its strength, some Ottoman officials sought to modernise the Empire by adopt-ing Western measures. Modernization started with the military and resulted in the abolition of the Janissaries, a form of Imperial Guard that had long dominated the Ottoman military establishment, in the early nineteenth century. In order to protect its integrity, the Ottoman Empire started to grant freedom to minorities through imperial decrees issued in 1839 and 1856, with this period becoming known as the Tanzimat (Reform) Era. In the case of American missionaries, until they were recognized by the Sublime Porte, they carried out their activities under the protection of the British but, over time, through imperial charters, American missionaries started to strengthen their foreigner status. The Tanzimat reforms also had an impact on the legal and political system of the Empire with the first Ottoman Constitution being adopted in 1876. Under this constitution a parliamentary system was introduced which brought the Sultan's abso-lute power under external control. However, in 1878 the Sultan regained his power and suspended the constitution. In 1908, alongside the Young

Turks' Revolution, constitutional government was re-introduced. All of these political and social changes had an influence upon the work of the missionaries. The Ottoman Empire regarded education as one of the most significant institutions in terms of its potential to transform society. This study argues that American missionary schools in the Ottoman Empire offered one of the best education systems. Therefore, Ottoman officials who saw the necessity of adopting a Western approach to education, collaborated with American missionaries and supported the missionaries in their establishment of a range of educational establishments from primary and military schools to seminaries and colleges. For example, William Goodell, who was the first missionary to arrive in Istanbul in 1831, opened a series of Lancastrian schools. He was asked by the Sublime Porte to open schools for the military, so they would have literate army officers. Two schools were opened in the first year, then seven military schools added and they were all being run by missionaries who provided all the text books from their own presses. This study further suggests that as a product of the American missionary establishment, Robert College is considered one of the most successful American institutions that modernised the Turkish educational system. The college, through its spread of American values, was able to train students who, after their graduation, continued to reflect the college's success. Influential figures such as Turkish Prime ministers Tansu Ciller (the only female prime minister to date) and Bülent Ecevit, not to mention Nobel Prize Winner Orhan Pamuk, graduated from Robert College. The main title of the study is "From Empire to Republic" because this book analyzes American missionary enterprise from its establishment within the Ottoman Empire in the nineteenth century to the foundation of the Turkish Republic in 1923. In order to limit its scope the book will focus on the educational aspect of the ABCFM and will specifically deal with Robert College.

In the first chapter, this book will look at missionary theories in order to understand the philosophy of American missionaries. It will examine American missionaries and the foundation of the American Board of Commissioners for Foreign Missions. The second chapter will explain the actual arrival of missionaries in the Ottoman Empire. The third chapter will give an account of early American and Ottoman relations. The fourth chapter will explain the work of American missionaries in Anatolia. The final chapter deals with Robert College.

1 The Origins of American Protestant Missionaries

> Go ye into all the world and preach the gospel to every creature. Mark 16:15.

A missionary is a person whose aim is to spread their religion to the inhabitants of foreign countries with the term generally being used for Christians. The term *mission* originates from the Latin *missio* which means despatching or sending, amongst other things (Aydın 2005). The term not only means assignment, but mission is also used in reference to the institutions that Christians have established. The earliest missionary activities can be traced back to the Saints or original disciples of Jesus (Cilacı 1982). The history of missionary undertaking can be divided into five time periods: Saints Era (33–100); Church Establishment Era (100–800); Middle Ages Era (800–1500); Reformation Era (1500–1650); Post Reformation Era (1650–1800); Modern Era (1800-Today) (Kocabasoglu 2000, in Taskin 2007: 31).

Saint Paul is considered one of the pioneers of Christian missionaries. He established churches in Anatolia, Macedonia and Greece in order to spread Christianity. In the sixth century, Saint Augustinus sent preachers to the Anglo-Saxons. In the eighth century, Saint Bonifacius tried to spread Christianity throughout Rhein. Charlemagne's victories also led to the Saxons' acceptance of Christianity. In the ninth century, Germanic people started to embrace Christianity, and in the same century, Christianity became widespread in Sweden and Bohemia. In the tenth century, Christianity started to be accepted in Denmark and Christian missions emerged in Russia, Prussia and Hungary. With German and Scandinavian acceptance of Christianity, and the Roman Catholic Church's dominance over Europe, missionaries' activities gained importance. With regard to the military aspect of such missionary activity, whilst the Crusades may have halted the spread of Islam to Europe, they did not result in the conversion of Muslims. Franciscan and Dominican monks were among the first groups who embraced missionary activities with some of their number going to Asia for their work. Rev. Josiah Strong further adds that "the Eastern nations sink, their glory ends, And Empire rises where the sun descends," hence the United States, with its vast resources, population, economic strength, and Protestant faith saw itself as the leader in civilizing and evangelizing the world (Strong 1885, in Shelton 2011: 22).

It has been claimed that missionaries, and in particular Protestant missionaries, have connections to capitalism in that missionaries, through their work, not only spread their religion, but also the economic and social policies of their country of origin. The Protestant faith paid particular attention to missionary work and, after some major developments that took place within the Protestant church, they started building missionary stations. Modern missionary activities started with the establishment of the Baptist Missionary Society in 1792 in London by William Carey, who went to India in 1793. A few years later, in 1797, the Netherlands Missionary Society was established. The whole of the 19th century, together with the first quarter of the 20th, was the golden age of missionary enterprise. This period coincides with capitalism overtaking imperialism, with missionary activities being considered as a significant factor contributing to this change (Kocabasoglu 2000, in Taskin 2007: 42). Among the many forms of Christian faith, Protestantism would seem the best fit with regard to capitalism. Many branches of the Protestant faith emerged when the capitalist movement started to become more widespread. Protestant belief was especially popular in the commercial and early industrialized cities. For example, in the sixteenth century, most wealthy urban centers already had Protestant dwellers (Weber 1997). In another example, the followers of "God Give Me Money" believed that Protestantism and Capitalism had sacred bounds (Danacıoglu 1993).

Protestantism contributed to the translation of the Bible into foreign languages, emphasized the practice of religion in the national tongue and the importance of a national church. According to Max Weber, the values that Protestantism signifies facilitated capital saving and thus improved the lives of the bourgeois and capitalists (Kıslalı 2003). According to the Protestant faith, success and work are the means of practicing one's religion. In order to gain God's favor, people need to work hard and in return God helps them to become rich. Protestants moreover are against luxury and prodigality. Another Weberian approach suggests that the reason why Islamic countries lag behind the capitalist nations is because of their religious belief.

According to this belief Christianity promotes capitalism, whereas Islam prevents its development (Kıslalı 2003).

The opponents of this view suggest that there is no direct relationship between Protestantism and capitalism and in reality modern capitalism is not a result of any particular religion. According to Baykan Sezer, in the light of Max Weber, a relation can be constructed between Judaism and capitalism. At the same time, a bourgeois attitude and Catholicism can harmoniously work together as can be seen from French literature. Thus, he concludes that it is not true that religions influence economic developments (Sezer 1981, in Taskin 2007: 43). Samir Amin points out that, Christianity did not promote capitalism; it is capitalism that promoted Christianity (Amin 1993, in Taskin 2007: 43).

American Protestant missionary initiatives originate from what was termed the First and Second Great Awakening. The First Great Awakening aimed at evangelizing people in the American continent, with the Second Great Awakening being focused on converting people abroad. The First Awakening sought to embed religion in the daily lives of the people and to reach people from all social classes. Jonathan Edwards is considered one of the pioneers of the movement; through his sermons he supported the ideas of salvation by God, predestination and "intimate and individual religious experience with God" (Devrim 2014). In his sermons, he asked his audience to practice their religion in an active manner. He encouraged people to discover religion themselves. He endorsed the idea of "revival of religion and the advancement of Christ's kingdom on earth" (Edwards 1747, in Devrim 2014:18). The Second Great Awakening promoted the concept of individualism and supported "socio-religious mobilization" at home and abroad. From this many Americans understood that it was their destiny to serve and act as a model to spread the gospel.

It is also important to note that both of these movements gained the support of females and they became active missionaries. Many of them came from the lower strata of society and progressed to being active members of churches, and occupying positions in philanthropic, relief and missionary organizations. They started to work at both home and abroad. They also replaced their husband's work when they went to foreign missions. When women did go abroad, they worked as midwives, nurses, teachers, instructors and missionaries (Morgan 1966, Henretta 1973;

in Devrim 2014: 20). Helen Barrett Montgomery states that by 1909, the women's missionary societies raised \$3,328,840 (up from \$115 the first year); they supported 2,368 women missionaries in the field; 3,263 schools overseas of which 2,410 were in villages and 11 were colleges; and the organization had published over 63 million pages of literature, including a 10-volume series of books that had sold over 600,000 copies. There were, in 1909, 815,596 contributing members (Montgomery 1910, in Shelton 2011: 26). R. Pierce Beaver states that missionary work constructed the core of all women's activities in churches and in their communities of origin. He further states that: "No other form of American intervention overseas has made a more powerful cultural impact than this work for women and children" (Beaver 1968, in Shelton 2011: 11). In addition, he adds that the Women's Foreign Mission Movement can be considered as the First Feminist Movement. Missionary societies instructed women how to organise, raise their own voices and improve themselves in professional life. For example, one of the most influential woman missionaries was Mary Lyon who established Mount Holyoke College in 1837. Dana Robert states that missionary women had an influence on their church community. In 1800, missionary women started to reform their churches, especially conservative evangelical churches. She said that missionaries altered the role of women in their own communities (Robert 2002, in Shelton 2011: 28). Missionary women were perceived as saints, martyrs, and as heroines who promoted women's leadership. Women constituted about 60 percent of the mission force and they constructed social and cultural bridges between the United States and their host countries. In time, women's missionary work gained an imperialistic character. Missionary women increased their work on education, sanitation and medicine.

Millennialism is considered another significant element of the missionary movement. It supports the idea that the end of the world is approaching and the Kingdom of God would soon be established. Puritans also believed that after a thousand years of Christ's reign, an apocalyptic end would take place. In this period, it is also observed that there is a transition from pre-millennialism to millennialism which asserts that a thousand years of peace would be followed by the Second Coming of Christ. In short, millennialism is one of the most significant concepts that contributed to the spread of missionary work in foreign lands. Other voluntary institutions, apart from churches, individuals, bible associations, tract societies, women's and children's groups also contributed to missionary work in the USA. Such organisations gathered people from different classes and social backgrounds who worked towards a collective mission. In one of ABCFM's documents it is stated that "this free, open, responsible Protestant form of association, embracing both sexes, and all classes and ages, the masses of the people, is peculiar to modern times. It could not have worked, could not have existed, even, with sufficient energy for the conversion of the world, without facilities for intercommunication among the nations, civil and religious liberty, extended habits of reading, and a wide-spread intelligence" (ABCFM Memorial Volume 299, in Shelton 2011: 38). One of the most significant aspects of missionary work is its contribution to social, cultural and scientific exchange between countries. Missionaries took their Western ideals in terms of education, medicine and social life to their host countries. In return, they also educated themselves in the languages, geography, archeology, anthropology and ethnology of the country in which they were working. Furthermore, American missionaries not only spread Christianity, but also the American lifestyle and values. They drew their values from the Bible, the Declaration of Independence and the US Constitution. They fervently supported the concepts of freedom; the foundation of nation as a society based on law; individual achievement through hard work and the dignity of manual labor; the necessity of education which allowed literate people to read the Bible; respect for women and the desirability of education for women; personal integrity through honesty, virtue, and righteous living; inventiveness and harnessing technology for improvements in economic conditions and welfare. They aimed at advancement towards perfection whether for an individual or a society, of the value of change to bring improvements to peoples' lives (Shelton 2011: 195–96).

Robert E. Speer states that in 1902, both European and American missionaries had 558 missionary societies throughout the world; including 8,700 missionaries, 79,400 native workers, 7,320 mission stations, 14,364 churches, 94 colleges and universities, 20,458 schools, 379 hospitals, 782 dispensaries, 152 publishing houses, 452 translations of the Bible, and sixty-four ships. According to Speer the annual income of all the missionary societies stood at more than $20 million (Shelton 2011: 41).

1.1 The establishment of the American Board of Commissioners for Foreign Missions

Samuel J. Mills, Jr., James Richards, Gordon Hall, Luther Rice, Adoniram Judson, Samuel Nott, and Samuel Newell are important figures in the formation of American missionary work abroad. They were students who had all graduated from colleges that were constructed during the Second Great Awakening. Four of these students established a secret organisation called the "Society of Brethren" which is associated with "The Brethren." The group's aim was to construct a Christian mission abroad and to this end they sought the support of their professors at Andover College. The students collaborated with the "reverend fathers" in the meeting of the General Association of Massachusetts Proper at Bradford. In the meeting, the students said that they were interested in constructing a mission abroad to evangelize the heathen. Their demand received a positive answer from Hall and Rice. The Board of Commissioners for Foreign Missions was approved at Bradford and was established in Boston by members of the Congregational, Presbyterian and Reformed churches in 1810. It was the first foreign mission board established in the United States, as well as being the largest in the nineteenth century. The mission reflected New England traditions and aimed at spreading evangelical Protestant values, an inquisitive educational system, and American culture from food habits to family relations, and more important, the representation of an evangelical Protestant christianity. Missionaries considered their mission as "the most stupendous undertaking, which has ever been conceived by men, which in fact, could never have been conceived by men apart from divine revelation and command" (Patton 1924, in Sahin 2004: 19). Missionaries based upon Puritan teaching also believed that the United States was the most civilized country in the world and thus it was the missionaries' task to spread evangelical Protestant Christianity.

The board held its first meeting in Farmington, Connecticut, in September 1810 and assigned Samuel Worcester who was a pastor of the Tabernacle Congregational Church in Salem, Massachusetts as corresponding secretary. The Prudential Committee, a smaller executive committee under the direction of the Board, was established and a constitution was adopted. The Board first aimed at converting native Americans and Catholics on the

American continent. However, they soon broadened their aim as being to evangelize the whole world. Their motto was "the field is the world" (Yucel 2012: 52). Their methodology included distribution of Holy Scriptures and explaining their meaning (First Ten Annual Reports 67, in Dogan 2013: 30). In the year 1810–11, the ABCFM collected $999.52 (Shelton 2011: 56). Moreover, the missionaries' newspaper, the *Missionary Herald*, started to be published in 1818, an outgrowth of the earlier Panoplist, as a monthly pamphlet of 32 pages. The Board first assigned missionaries to Calcutta and Burma. However, because of the Anglo-American War in 1812 and disagreements between American and British officials, they soon decided to divert their efforts to Jerusalem as it was the "principal birth place of Christianity" (Yücel 2012: 53). The Board's income grew about 50% in the 1820s, then tripled in the 1830s and stabilized in the 1840s at about $250,000. By the end of that decade, income had grown to nearly $300,000 (Shelton 2011: 56).

2 Arrival of Missionaries in the Ottoman Empire

The Ottoman Empire was always multicultural, inhabited by people from different religious and ethnic backgrounds, and thus attractive to foreigners. This attraction arose from the Ottoman Empire's tolerance of non-Muslims, together with capitulations and privileges offered to foreigners. In the case of the Ottoman Empire's legal administrative and legal system, it was bound to the Padishah (Sultan) and Shariah law. In this context, from the sixteenth century, the Empire attracted British, French, Swedish, German and American missionaries. There were a number of reasons why Christians, Jews and Muslims were interested in the territory. As the Empire started to decline and central authority began to lose its power, the missionary work gained an imperialistic character. One of the most significant reasons why missionaries went to the Ottoman Empire was that it was occupying territories sacred to, or revered by, Christians. For example, Christian missionaries referred to Anatolia as "Bible Land" (Sezer 1999, Sisman 2002). It must be borne in mind that historically "Bible Land" was one of the most significant factors that initiated the Crusades. Therefore, it was important for Christians to reclaim the land via missionary work. In addition, the eastern question and the industrialized western countries seeking markets, were other reasons why the Ottoman Empire's territories gained importance (Taskin 2007: 34).

The first missionary group which is known to have started work in Istanbul was a group of Catholic Capuchin monks. They came to Istanbul in 1220 and were part of the Saint Francois branch of Franciscan missionaries. Today they are known as Conventuals. These missionaries came to Istanbul in order to merge the churches of Byzantium and Rome. In other words, they tried to spread the Catholic faith among the Greeks of Byzantium. Conventual priests established educational institutions. Their schools were constructed close to Latin churches and they continued their work by educating the children of Latin families (Polvan 1952). In the late sixteenth century, these French missionaries re-emerged in order to spread Christianity and support minorities in Istanbul (Turan 1999: 204). In 1583, Jesuits constructed a French school named St. Benoit. Apart from Jesuits, other

Catholic groups such as Franciscans, Dominicans, Capuchins and Friars started to come to the Ottoman Empire. They also established schools, namely: St. Joseph, St. Michel, St. Louis and Notre Dame de Sion. Jesuits and Franciscans formed densely populated groups in Istanbul, Izmir, Aleppo, Syria, Palestine, Egypt, Iraq and Cyprus. From the seventeenth century, the missionaries received the support of the Pope and utilised capitulations to increase their missionary activities. Apart from Catholics, Protestants also carried out missionary activities in Ottoman territories (Bliss 1908, in Taskin 2007: 35). Protestant missionary activities started under the aegis of British institutions. Then, in the early nineteenth century, Americans started to join the movement and they became the most active and influential missionary group. Some scholars argue that the first Protestant missionaries who came to the Ottoman Empire were part of the Brethren's Society for The Furtherance of The Gospel Among The Heathen. These missionaries tried to make contacts with the Ecumenical Patriarchate of Constantinople. Between 1768–1783, they started to work in Egypt (Turan 1999, in Taskin 2007: 36). Other scholars say that the first Protestant missionary came to Istanbul in 1815 and he was a member of the Church Missionary Society (Kocabasoglu 2000, in Taskin 2007: 36). English missionaries established stations in the Mediterranean. The Church Missionary Society (CMS), was established in 1799, began its operations in the Mediterranean in 1812 and set up a Mediterranean mission in Malta in 1815. Other British missionary organizations included the London Missionary Society, the British and Foreign Bible Society, the London Society for Promoting Christianity among the Jews, the Religious Tract Society, and the Wesleyan Methodists. The British missionaries assisted American missionaries with support and advice for the newly arriving American missionaries, and reports on British missionary work frequently appeared in the columns of the missionary periodicals in the United States during the 1820s (Dogan 2013: 6).

2.1 The Millet System

In order to understand the Ottoman Empire's social and political structure, it is important to grasp the significance of the millet system, which was based upon Shariah law. In Islam, the concept of *millet* means religion or sect together with a community that is bound to a particular religion or sect. In one Ottoman dictionary known as *Kamus-i Türki*, the terms "religion" and "millet" are synonymous. However, in the case of "millet" and "community" there is a difference. In the Ottoman Empire, *millet* meant a group of persons who are bound to a religion. As Islam was the 'official' religion of the Empire, people were divided into believers and non-believers, with the latter divided into millets along religious lines (Bozkurt 1989). However, following the French Revolution, the Ottoman Empire started to change the millet system from its original religious basis to a system of categorization based on nation. In other words, non-muslims under Ottoman rule were originally categorized according to their sect or religion and these groups were called millet. Categorization of minorities according to their nations was not applicable until the end of the nineteenth century. In the millet system every religious group's leader was responsible for their own community. The millet system was officially recognized by Ottoman officials and they were religious communities that had limited authority within their own groups (Kennedy 2008: 16). There were for example, Muslim, Greek-Orthodox, Armenian, Jewish and Catholic nations (*millet*) within the Ottoman population. The Sublime Porte categorized the Ottoman subjects according to their religion, with non-Muslims being divided into two groups: Christians and Jews. The former was further divided into two sub-groups, the first of which comprised Catholic Christians: Latins, Georgians, Armenians, Assyrians, Maronites, Copts and Catholic Greeks. The second group was non-Catholics: Orthodoxes, Gregorians, Nestorians and Melchites. In the case of Jews, they were categorised as Qaraites and Rabbinics. Apart from Shariah Law, minorities' rights and properties were determined by capitulations and agreements.

2.2 The Tanzimat and Islahat Decrees and the first Ottoman Constitution

The most significant aspect of the Decrees and the first Ottoman Constitution is their promotion of human rights and westernization. The reforms affected the work of missionaries who started to spread their ideas in a more overt fashion. In time, Protestant missionaries gained a new non-Muslim foreigners' status in the Empire. The Tanzimat (reform) era stretched from 1839–76, beginning when Sultan Abdulmecit issued the Imperial Edict of

Gulhane in 1839. The edict's aim was to modernize the Empire by adopting European measures in social and political fields. The Gulhane decree assured the life, honor and property of people in the Empire regardless of their faith and ethnicity and guaranteed religious freedoms of minority groups. The edict's aim was to prevent any foreign influence within its boundaries as well as to reorganize the legal status of the millet. In its Annual Report of 1840, the ABCFM states that soon after the young Sultan came to the throne, a charter of rights was granted to the people, without their asking for it, providing for some fundamental changes in the internal administration of the government. In the presence of all foreign ambassadors, the sovereign solemnly pledged himself to guard, as far as in him lay, the liberty, prosperity and honor of every individual subject, without reference to his religious creed (ABCFM 1840, in Shelton 2011: 208).

The decree offered a new system of taxation in order to abolish the corruption and unfair burdens of the earlier system of tax farming. In the case of modernizing the armed forces, the decree constructed a new method of recruiting and sustaining the military. Missionary Dwight added that: "Under this very charter, changes the 'most momentous,' particularly for the Christian and Jewish populations, have already taken place in Turkey; according to the honest intentions and policy of the present government, there is ultimately to be a complete carrying out of its provisions in every part of the empire" (ABCFM 1840, in Shelton, 2011: 209). In addition, the edict stated that in the new system governors and ruling pashas throughout the empire would receive a salary from the government, rather than depending on tax collections for their well-being (ABCFM 1840, in Shelton 2011: 209) With regard to the imperial edict, Cyrus Hamlin said that: "The true value of this document is to be sought in its effects upon the people more than in the administration of government. It went through the empire. It woke up the slumbering East. It was the first voice that announced to the people the true subject of government, and the legitimate ends to be obtained" (Hamlin 2014).

Hamlin further added that the most significant contribution of the decree would be that it would permit the opening of a Protestant school. The reforms in the Empire were not welcomed by all strata of society. English historian Sir John A. R. Marriott pointed out that Reshit Pasha was the leader of reform and was the Turkish ambassador to France and England.

He had been influenced by Western ideals and was supported by Sultan Mahmud and his successor Abdulmecit. However, after its announcement, Reshit Pasha faced reactions from some members of the Ulema – a body of Muslim scholars who are recognized as having specialist knowledge of Islamic sacred law and theology – as they called him infidel. They found the reforms to be "blasphemous violation of the Koran" and "contrary to the fundamental law of the Ottoman Empire," and that they were merely an attempt to put Moslem and Christian on an equal footing. They feared that the reforms would promote unrest among the subject populations and encourage perpetual agitation (Marriott 1966: 248–51). However, because there was no Protestant millet recognized by the Porte, those who converted to Protestantism were losing their official identity. Therefore, even though missionaries were able to open schools during the early 1840s, because of their lack of millet status, they did not have legal or civil protection. The Protestant converts were excommunicated by their former churches, turned out by their families and friends, and were outside any portion of society.

As the number of American Protestant missionaries increased in the Ottoman Empire, it contributed to the emergence of the Protestant Armenian community as a religious millet. With the support of William Goodell, American missionary, together with Sir Stratford Canning and Lord Stratford de Redcliffe, the British ambassadors to Istanbul, Sultan Abdulmecit issued an imperial decree which recognized the Protestant community in the Empire. Upon the announcement of this policy, the American Board's foreign secretary, Rufus Anderson, stated: "We owe all this, under God, to the providential fact that England had gained an empire in India, and must needs preserve an unencumbered way to it" (Anderson 1872). William Goodell said: "We love to consider your Lordship's influence as one of the important providential means by which God has been pleased to carry on His work" (Prime 1876). In 1850, another imperial decree granted the native Protestants millet status. It placed evangelical Christians on the same legal status as other Christian communities in the empire (Kennedy 2008: 30). The decree was considered as a charter of religious liberty. The imperial edict of 1850 was reinforced through the edict of 1853.

After the outbreak of the Crimean war and the Treaty of Paris (1856), the Ottoman Empire was formally recognized by the European states. Its integrity was guaranteed by the treaty and its European signatories.

Following these developments, the Ottoman Sultan issued the Imperial Rescript of Reform of 1856. The millet system was abolished on paper and the edict recognized the subjects of the Ottoman Empire as citizens and stipulated religious equality before the law to all the sultan's subjects. In other words, the edict provided freedom of conscience and religious profession to all Ottoman subjects. Protestants maintained their rights as citizens of the Ottoman state. After the edict of 1856, American missionaries easily regulated their printing presses, hospitals, educational and religious centers. The number of Muslim converts also gained some small momentum. For example, Edward Williams, started preaching and baptizing Turks. Selim Efendi who was an Istanbul citizen converted to Christianity. Another convert case was that of Shemseddin who was an Imam and had memorized the Koran. Then, he started his studies in a missionary college in Izmir (Harlow 1919: 13–25). In its 1856 Annual Report, the ABCFM stated that "...the most interesting part of the report is that which gives us official evidence, through our Minister at Constantinople, that the Turkish government has granted complete toleration to all its subjects, Muslim as well as Christian. This is not merely a religious change, but a political revolution. It is one of the wonders of the age; and we have reason to exclaim in view of it, 'What hath God wrought!'" The Report further added: "The Armenian mission embraces a wide and most promising field of labor, ripe or fast ripening for the harvest... and was never, on the whole, in a better working condition than at present; and never had brighter prospects of success in extending the knowledge of a pure gospel among the Armenian people" (ABCFM 1856: 21–22). As stated above, before Protestants were recognized as a distinct millet by the Ottoman Government, those who converted to Protestantism were losing their official identity. Thus, there was no authority representing them (Erhan 2000). In order to be recognized, American missionaries under the British Embassy and the United States Legation initiated an intensive campaign aimed at the Sublime Porte (Erhan 2000: 324). Furthermore, according to Ottoman officials, there was no difference between American and British missionaries. They were co-operating together for "common humanity". Their solidarity is based upon their shared language and culture (Dogan 2013: 49). In the case of education the edict stated that: "All of the subjects of my Empire, without distinction, shall be received into the Civil and Military Schools of the Government, if they otherwise satisfy the conditions as to age and examination which are specified in the Organic Regulations of the said Schools. Moreover, every community is authorized to establish Public Schools of Science, Art, and Industry. Only the method of instruction and the choice of Professors in schools of this class shall be under the control of a Mixed Council of Public Instruction, the members of which shall be named by sovereign command" (Stone 2006: 23). Some missionaries said that, thanks to the edicts, Christians and Jews can "enjoy the same privileges as the Turk" (Temple 1855: 246–7).

Furthermore, Sultan Abdulmecit with regard to the edicts stated: "It is my imperial desire that no improper or disorderly thing of whatever kind, be thoughtlessly occasioned to the faithful subjects of my kingdom of the Protestant faith, and that the special privileges granted by my Imperial Government concerning religion and matters pertaining to it, be perpetually preserved from all detriment. And, as it is my imperial will that no injury of whatever kind, or in whatever manner, come upon them, therefore, this most righteous imperial edict has been written, that those against it, may know that, exposing themselves to my royal indignation, they shall be punished" (Dwight 1854, in Dogan 2013: 83).

On the other hand, Protestant missionaries, the Ottoman government, the Eastern Churches and European countries would all seem to have a different interpretation of these two edicts. For example, some missionaries conceived the edicts as granting total religious liberty to the people which would mean that they were free to choose whichever religion they wanted to follow. Moreover, William Goodell who was a missionary, said before the decrees were issued that the missionaries were subject to oppression more often (Dogan 2013: 84). ABCFM missionaries further stated that Protestant communities gained a more secure situation following the edicts in comparison to other Christian groups who were supported by European countries. Some Christians believed that the imperial decrees would mean that Muslims could also convert to Christianity if they wanted to do so (Dogan 2013: 86). Before the decrees were issued, it was not possible for Muslims to change their religion, and even after the decree was issued there were only few cases where Muslims converted. After the Congress of Berlin in 1878, the European countries also endorsed reforms that would improve the status of Christians and particularly the Armenians. However, when Sultan Abdulhamit ascended to the throne, many of the liberties were curtailed. The first Ottoman Constitution (*Kanun-i Esasi*) of 1876 is one of the most significant legal documents that regulated systems within the Ottoman Empire. Its eight articles suggested that "everybody under the Ottoman allegiance, irrespective of his religion and sect, is identified as Ottoman without an exception." This gave Protestants, as well as other sects, full equality in the Empire.

3 Early Ottoman-American Relations

Before American interest started in the Ottoman Empire, a long standing European impact can be seen to have existed. When the first Sultan of the Empire, Mehmet II, conquered Constantinople in 1453, he inherited colonies of Genoese and Florentines. Their compatriots could also be found in ports along the country's coastline, with these communities being vital for trading purposes. Keen to make its mark in an international arena, the Ottoman Empire continued existing commercial relationships and began to develop new diplomatic relations. In 1535, the Empire granted its first capitulations. This means it granted rights and privileges to foreigners who dwelt in the empire (Kennedy 2008: 15).

Early American-Ottoman encounters date back to the Barbary Wars which took place during 1801–05 and 1815–16. The wars raised the question of the protection of American citizens. At that time, the American government could not protect its citizen-sailors. When their vessels were captured, they were sent into slavery and relatives of those captives petitioned the American government to pay ransoms. However, the government was unable to pay anything as the national coffers were empty at that time. The American sailors' captivity led to a debate over whether there should be a branch of the national navy to protect American shipping. In 1815, American sailors gained their freedom with the support of the American Navy and the Marines. In 1823, the United States started to follow the Monroe Doctrine which stipulated that the United States would not tolerate foreign intervention. The USA opened consulates instead of embassies around the world. The commercial interests of Americans in North Africa led to a new treaty with Ottomans. On February 8, 1830, the Treaty of Amity and Commerce was signed between the United States and the Ottoman Empire (Gordon 1932). With this treaty, the USA obtained a new status and its ships were allowed access to the Black Sea via the Bosphorus Straits. For its part the United States agreed to assist the Ottomans with the building of warships and to give them the necessary American timber.

In 1831 Commodore David Porter, himself a veteran of the Barbary Wars, was appointed as the first American *charge d'affaires* in Istanbul and then gained the status of minister resident. The American missionaries had a significant impact on US-Ottoman relations, even acting as unofficial advisors to the American Consulates. However, their protection as well as that of their properties in the Empire was one of the most significant issues. The Act of Incorporations which contributed to the establishment of the Board stated: "that missionaries who are spreading the Gospel to foreign countries are engaging in lawful and proper work for American clergy. The American government issues passports to American missionaries the same as they do for all American citizens. These passports entitle all American citizens to equal protection by their government; the passports declare them to be American citizens who should be respected by foreign governments" (Shelton 2011: 240). Commodore David Porter was the first official US representative in the Ottoman Empire. David Finnie asserts that Porter was "…much less inclined than some of his European colleagues to take energetic action and more likely to think up reasons why nothing could be done" if asked to intervene with the Porte (Finnie 1967: 127). In 1841, David Porter was requested by the Sublime Porte to order American missionaries to leave the territory in Mount Lebanon because their presence there concerned the Maronite Patriarch. In his response to this request he wrote: "The Constitution of the United States allows to all its citizens the right of free exercise of their religious opinions, but no article of the Treaty of Commerce and Navigation between the United States and Turkey gives them authority to interfere in any way with the rites and religion of any person living under the authority of Turkey; therefore after this correspondence has been made known to the American citizens residing in the vicinity of Mount Lebanon, any attempt to excite the minds of the inhabitants to change their rites and religion must be done at their own risk, and on their responsibility" (Finnie 1967: 127). This means that American officials there had limited representation and thus could neither protect Americans nor ask them to leave the country. In return, the Sublime Porte stated that the government could not guarantee the safety of Americans and they had to leave the country soon. The Commodore then stated that he had no authority to remove the missionaries but that he could only inform them. Therefore, before Commodore Porter actively protected the missionaries, they were supported by American war vessels and fire power (Shelton 2011: 240). American missionaries asked American representatives to act in the matter of their damaged properties. They also asked Ottoman officers to intervene when problems occurred in the country (Porter 1875). The AB-CFM re-emphasized the concept of missionary work. It stated that the missionaries were supported by the American government; they were only American citizens. Their missions were not permanent as they expected to return to their homeland when they had finished their labors. They did not expect to become citizens of the countries in which they dwelt. In the case of their children, they were also American citizens and at some point would be sent back to the USA for their education. In 1843, Dabney Carr, took over from David Porter. He took a firmer stance in terms of protecting American missionaries. In a letter to the American consul in Beirut he wrote: "The missionaries themselves know that I will protect them to the full extent of my power, not only through you but, if need be, by calling the whole of the American squadron in the Mediterranean to Beyrout" (U.S. National Archives 1848, in Shelton 2011: 243). It should be borne in mind that the lack of protection impaired the work of the missionaries. Goodell said: "Those to whom we have preached the Gospel or to whom we have sold the Scriptures, or with whom we have communed at the table of the Lord, may be thrown into dungeons, or otherwise harassed, and we may be unable to obtain any official interference in their behalf" (Shelton 2011: 245). He further stated that official representatives have limited power due to their treaty. Missionaries identified the scarce number of American representatives in the inner parts of the Ottoman Empire as another problem. They contended that there were not enough American officials to guarantee required actions are taken by the Ottoman government, and that American missionaries and their families are thereby not protected. Missionaries further added that they had to deal with local authorities who were often reluctant to facilitate their work. For example, missionaries demanded the appointment of American Consuls at Erzroom and at Harpoot. However, it was only in 1886 that Mr. Jewett, who was himself the son of missionaries, was appointed to the interior of Turkey and he was based in Sivas. In the case of Harpoot, an American consulate was finally established there before the outbreak of the First World War. The missionaries then turned to the Department of State in Washington, suggesting that officials in Washington could urge the Minister resident in Constantinople, to increase his activities in the matter of protecting US citizens who resided in Turkey. This would involve the Minister in Constantinople in further contact with the Sublime Porte to try and secure the presence of US citizens (Shelton 2011: 249). Edwin de Leon, who was the American Consul in Alexandria, wrote to Washington and stated that if Ottoman Empire officials do not take immediate actions with regard to protection of the missionaries "American life and property will never...be safe in Syria, nor the American name respected" (U.S. National Archives 1858, in Shelton 2011: 250).

In 1859, the Navy sent the USS Macedonian to the Syrian coast and the Resident Minister in Constantinople, James Williams, was ordered by the State Department to show the flag. Before the treaty was signed the United States was not officially recognized by the Porte. American citizens, including the missionaries, carried out their activities in Ottoman lands under the British Embassy in Istanbul and through British consulates located in various cities of the Empire. For instance, "...the missionaries in Beirut received, travel permits from the *Porte*, through the British Consulate in that town. This method was valid for those who came to Istanbul before the American Legation was opened" (Goodell 1883, in Erhan 2000: 317). Moreover, the Sublime Porte put British and American missionaries, as well as the members of English speaking Protestant churches, into same group as British. Therefore, Americans had the same privileges as the British. However, when the 1830 treaty was signed missionaries as well as other American citizens lost their privilege of being "British" subjects before the Ottoman court. However, because of the American Legation's weak influence and the limited number of American consulates around the Empire, American missionaries continued to have close relationships with British diplomats to secure their presence in Ottoman lands. In 1842, at the ABCFM Board meeting in January, it was emphasized that American missionaries were entitled to be protected as they represented a distinct and important part of any American community. Missionaries had the same rights as any other profession. Their duties led them to work overseas in order to spread Christianity to all people, including the heathen, the infidel and all those in un-evangelized parts of the world. American missionaries were acting on behalf of all those members and institutions in the United States.

4 American Missionaries' Arrival in Anatolia

The work of Protestant missionaries in the Ottoman Empire increased by the middle of the nineteenth century because of the Empire's decreasing power and the growth in imperialism among the western countries. Missionaries became more active in Istanbul, Izmir and Jerusalem and their work soon took on a political character due to the increasing colonization movement. It is important to note that Catholic groups in the Ottoman Empire were supported by France and Austria, with the Orthodox being endorsed by Russia. In the case of Protestants, they were supported by Britain. For example, in 1840 Britain asked permission from the Porte to construct a Protestant missionary church in Jerusalem. In the beginning, the Porte declined this request. However, in 1842 the Porte allowed the construction of the church. Missionaries in that area made their first contacts with the Druze (Vahapoglu 2005). In 1846, there were four Protestant churches in the whole of Anatolia.

Pliny Fisk and Levi Parsons were the first American missionaries assigned to proselytize in the Ottoman Empire. They were both graduates of Williams College and Andover Theological Seminary. The *Missionary Herald* stated that their objective was to spread: "...the Gospel to Jews and Muslims" and awaken Christians in America "to the duties of the times" (ABCFM 1819, in Kennedy 2008: 11). With regard to settling in Jerusalem, Levi Parson stated that American Protestants should: "...restore the Jews to their rightful place in the Holy Land" (ABCFM 1878, in Kennedy 2008: 11). They should not, however, act like crusaders. Furthermore: "In no man is knowledge more really power than the schoolmaster," the Prudential Committee of the ABCFM said to a departing missionary, "and by none is it more valued, by none more certainly used" (Salt 2002: 290).

Parsons and Fisk gathered $2,932.31 for their mission and in November 1819 they set out for Jerusalem, Palestine. With regard to settling in Jerusalem, some missionaries stated that "...after ages of darkness, the light of the gospel is soon to re-illumine the shores of Palestine..." (The Boston Recorder 1818, in Dogan 2013: 32). Another missionary stated that: "The glory of the Lord will return. The Jews are to be gathered in from their dispersions, and acknowledge Jesus, whom their fathers crucified, to be their Savior and their God. I consider this mission a grand link in the chain of events, which are preparatory to the second coming of our blessed Lord" (The Weekly Recorder 1819, in Dogan 2013: 32).

Furthermore, Edward Bliss stated: "It seemed intolerable to its founders that Christianity's birthplace should be forever in the grip of Islam, or left to exhibit a form of Christianity, ancient and well-established, but for the most time lifeless" (Strong 1910, in Devrim 2014: 24).

American missionaries believed that Ottoman Turkey, especially Istanbul, was strategically important as it was the "… political and economic capital, and social and cultural hub of the Near East, from where the Gospel light, faith and wisdom would radiate" (Barlett 2015). According to missionaries of the ABCFM, Christians in the Ottoman Empire were mere "nominal Christians" and they did not represent the true form of Christianity. Therefore, they believed that it was the duty of the American missionaries to become an example of their religion (Dogan 2013: 34). Missionaries said that their mission in Istanbul would lead to reformation of the nominal churches and revolution in the intellectual, social and cultural spheres of the country. Moreover, missionaries believed that their Puritan doctrine and experience gave them "intellectual elitism" that would be adopted by Ottoman subjects (Sahin 2004: 21). The Ottoman Empire was a strategically important place as it hosted the very first established churches of Christianity as well as the birth place of many apostles such as Paul, not to mention it is the place where the Bible was compiled (Devrim 2014: 25).

On January 15, 1820, Fisk and Parsons reached Izmir (*Smyrna*) to start their work. Izmir is a port city where Americans frequently visited for commercial exchange and a number of Americans, as well as a British Consulate, could be found in the city. Therefore, it was a good starting point for the Americans to begin their mission. The American Board's instruction was as follows: they were asked to make observation of the social class system in the Ottoman lands as well as neighboring countries. In addition they were asked to think upon the following: "The two grand inquiries ever present in your minds will be, 'What good can be done?' and 'By what means?' What can be done for the Jews? What for the pagans? What for the Mohammedans? What for the Christians? What for the people in Palestine?

What for those in Egypt, in Syria, in Armenia, in other countries to which your inquiry may be extended?" (Barton 1908: 119–120).

ABCFM further declared that missionaries went to Jerusalem "… as part of an extended and continually extending system of benevolent action for the recovery of the world to God, to virtue, and to happiness" (Field 1969: 93). Upon their arrival in Ottoman territory, some of the missionaries observed how people from different races, religions and social backgrounds lived together. The missionaries criticized the lack of established missionary stations in the Empire (Devrim 2014: 25). They further stated that people who lived in the coastal areas were more educated than the others inland, but still their number is very low. Stone highlights that people in the Ottoman Empire had lower literacy rates in comparison to the United States. For example, most of the Sultan's subjects were illiterate. The first official Ottoman newspaper was published in 1831 with publication of the first non-government newspaper following in 1840 (Stone 2006: 10). At this time in the US more than two thousand newspapers were being published. In addition, the United States had seventy nine colleges, twenty three medical schools and nine law schools.

In 1829, the Prudential Committee of the Board decided to establish a mission among Armenians in the Ottoman Empire. Eli Smith and Henry Otis Dwight were assigned to explore the field. They started their tour in the spring of 1830. In 1831 William Goodell was instructed to construct a new station in Istanbul (Erhan 2000: 318). He was chosen because of his "great organizational skills, deep evangelical religious attitudes and proficiency in Near Eastern Languages." When Goodell arrived in Istanbul there were half a million Turks, roughly 150,000 Greeks and Armenians, some 50,000 Jews, and a few thousand Europeans and other nationals. Istanbul became the center for all missionary activities in the Empire (Prime and Goodell 126–27, in Sahin 2004: 39).

American missionaries in the Ottoman Empire basically had four institutions: stations, churches, hospitals and schools and they started their work by first establishing churches (Kennedy 2008: 28). The missionaries used coffee houses, village rooms or house calls to spread their ideals (Akgün 1989). They observed that Turks were eager to learn about the Christian faith. However, because of pressure from their own religious figures, they could not convert. Meanwhile, missionaries in the Ottoman Empire demanded that more persons come to join them in the Empire, especially in the Mediterranean region, asserting that the political position of the country should not discourage others from visiting (ABCFM 1823: 125). In the Mediterranean as a whole most of the missionaries settled in Malta, Beirut, Jerusalem, and Izmir. The first official American Protestant church in Istanbul was founded in 1846. Its mission was to represent "true Christianity" and thus revitalize the Turkish Empire. However, they did not aim to "pull down or build up a sect, but to make known and inculcate the great fundamental truths of the Gospel" (The Missionary Herald 1830: 177). Instead, the American missionaries intended to proselytize only to "those who called upon them or whom they might meet as they went here and there" (Strong 1910: 92) The conservative attitude of Oriental churches also contributed to this approach. They adopted a simple, "non-ornamented and primitive form of Christianity" (Dodge 1972: 16). American missionaries also realized that it was not possible to approach Muslims unless the oriental churches changed their policies. American missionaries believed that the oriental churches' false representation of Christianity resulted in Muslims' developing prejudices against the religion. As was expressed in the *Missionary Herald*: "The worst obstacles which a missionary meets with are the contempt of Christianity or the prejudice against it, which the people feel, from having observed the immoral lives from countries nominally Christian, or from the unmeaning ceremonies, the bigotry, and the manifest hypocrisy of professedly Christian ministers and churches. The heathen, and so do the Muslims, easily see that such a religion has no good effect on the temper and conduct of its professors" (The Missionary Herald 1819–1870).

In the case of women in the Ottoman Empire, it was very rare for them to be literate, irrespective of their religion, and they did not normally play an active role in society. In the central cities, especially in Constantinople and Smyrna, there were educated women. In 1836, a school for girls was established in Smyrna. In 1845, the Female Seminary at Pera in Constantinople was opened with eight students. Miss Lovell, Mrs. Everett and Miss West became important figures in the education of girls in this school. In 1856, the American Board announced that it would no longer support missionary schools, rather it would focus on seminaries which trained native pastors. In the case of missionary schools, their only assignment would be preaching. The Board also made a clear statement regarding the work being undertaken in terms of spreading the religion vs. civilizing people. It stated: "We do not find, and the fact is to be noted, that Christ or his Apostles made any inventions or discoveries in the arts and sciences or sought directly to promote literature. We believe that the preaching of 'Christ and him crucified,' and that only, is sufficient to lead to the wisdom of God and the power of God unto salvation" (ABCFM 1856). In 1866, the Bible Women started to work in Constantinople. Their funds came from the American Bible Society and they were supported by Armenians. In 1860, Miss Myra A. Proctor established a Girls' Seminary in Aintab which is considered the oldest institution of its kind (Strong 1910: 222). In 1870 the American Board also constructed a female mission in the Ottoman Empire. However, because of the limited numbers of students, they could only become teachers and or work as nurses, but there was no female missionary who could preach. Then, Cora W. Tomson and Alexander Van Millingen came to Istanbul and initiated evangelistic visits and some preaching among the neighbors and pupils' parents. After the Woman's Boards of Mission was established, missionary work aimed specifically at women became more institutionalized. In 1872, the Girls' Boarding School at Constantinople was established by the Woman's Board of Missions. It started with only two students. After a couple of years, it became the American College for Girls at Constantinople.

A missionary, Miss Seymour, said that nearly all Americans in the Ottoman Empire were missionaries who had strong relations with the Armenian community. They also contributed to establishment of the First Armenian Evangelical Church, as some of the leaders of oriental churches were concerned about the "hypocrisy" and "superstition" that existed within the institution (Dodge 1972: 17). Dodge further highlights that American missionaries did not establish stations unless the local people asked them to do so. For example, the president of the Armenian National Council said to Mr. Dwight: "Now is the time for you to work for the Armenian people. Such an opportunity as you now enjoy may soon pass away and never more return. You should greatly enlarge your operations where you have one missionary, you should have ten; and where you have one book, you should put ten books in circulation" (Strong 1910: 197). American missionaries, even though they worked hard, believed that they could not totally satisfy their calling, with the Board at one point even asking them to stop their work with the Armenians. However, the reformation that took place in the Armenian church continued. For example, Tocat and Cesarea became significant missionary areas for Armenian missions especially during the years of 1854 and 1857. Mr. Dunmore stated that they needed forty more men as teachers and preachers in order to broaden their mission. In the 1860s, American missionaries became active in Kessab and Kilis (Strong 1910: 200).

American missionaries soon faced opposition from the Catholic Church as they were not happy about the spread of Protestantism. Roman Catholics were interested in educating Ottoman Greeks and thus they established the College of Saint Athanius in Rome and Jesuits established a school in Pera, Istanbul. They initiated exchange programs which were attended by boys from the Ottoman Empire. Cyrus Hamlin, who was the founder of the Bebek Seminary in Istanbul, said that the existence of Jesuit schools in the Empire threatened the existence of Protestant schools. He went on to say: "Give the two systems a fair trial, the Protestant and the Jesuit, in education; and if the Jesuit survives, let him survive. It is the survival of the fittest....If however, you have no schools or very inferior schools, the Jesuits will undoubtedly take the advantage offered them" (Stone 2006: 12).

Missionary activities increased after the opening of educational institutions. In the 1830s the Ottoman Empire supported the opening of schools in its territories and the Sultan at that time encouraged missionaries to provide materials. In 1850, the number of American churches was seven and there were seven missionary schools. In the next decade, the number of churches grew to forty-nine and there were one hundred and fourteen schools. By 1880, the number of churches had increased to ninety-seven and there were one hundred and thirty schools. In 1913, the number of churches reached one hundred and sixty three and there were four hundred and fifty missionary schools. In addition, the number of the Ottoman subjects attending those schools ranged from 13,095 in 1880 to 25,992 in 1913 (Grabill 1971). As schools developed, Turks realised that, for example, Armenian children attending those schools progressed better than their own children. Furthermore, Turks stated that they would prefer to send their children to American educational institutions. For example, the first Turkish girl graduated from the Istanbul Girls' College in 1890.

In the case of conversion, Fisk and Parsons stated that non-Muslims were allowed to convert if they wanted to do so. After interacting with the Jews, the missionaries understood that they were immune to proselytization. In 1849, missionary work started in Salonica aimed specifically at Jews. At that time it was estimated that there were 45,000 Sephardic Jews in Salonica, as well as large numbers of Askenazim (German) Jews, Sephardim (Spanish) Jews and Italian Jews in Constantinople. In the case of religious books, "nearly all Hebrew-Spanish Old Testaments printed in Vienna had been distributed, and the American Bible Society would underwrite the cost of a new edition to be printed in Smyrna" (ABCFM 1845: 85–6). Revs. E. M. Dodd and Justin Parsons said that the work would give more positive results if it had taken place in Bulgaria and Macedonia instead, asserting that Jews were reluctant to approach their religion. Moreover, they perceived English and Scottish missionaries were better able to do missionary work there. In the case of Muslims, because of Shariah law, the punishment for apostasy is death. Moreover, conversion would also lead to exclusion of persons from their own communities in economic and social terms. Indeed, changing one's religion was perceived as being equal to changing one's nationality (Kennedy 2008: 18) and when two Muslims converted in Central Turkey they were sent into exile by the Sublime Porte (Kennedy 2008: 18). In another example, the stations in Muscat, a city in Oman, converted only 5 Muslims over a period of fifty years (Neill 1986). Hence, the missionaries changed their policy and decided to evangelize Christians. This included the Greek and Arab Orthodox community, the Gregorian Armenians and Armenian Catholics, the Druze, the Nestorians and the Maronites who were Arab Catholics (Erhan 2000: 319). The missionaries did manage to convert small numbers of Christians, most of whom were poor and more or less dependent on the church (The Missionary Herald 1897: 398). In 1839, there were 800 Armenian converts to Protestantism (Erhan 2000: 321). The Gregorian church took a negative stance against American missionaries with the church excommunicating those Armenians who became Protestants. Such Protestant Armenian converts then faced obstacles in terms of their occupation if employed, and within all aspects of their daily lives and commercial activities. In addition, because Armenian converts were scattered over a wide area, they could not easily organize themselves against this action of the Gregorian church. Both the Orthodox Patriarchate and

Russia were also not happy with the work of the American missionaries. They expressed their discontent to the Sublime Porte (Ortaylı 1981).

The missionaries realized that the best method for spreading the gospel was to distribute holy books. Therefore, the ABCFM sent Daniel Temple to Malta to establish a mission printing press in 1822. He was assisted by the British and locals with the actual operation of the press. The American missionary printing press was called "The American Press" at the time of its establishment, later changing its name to "The Evangelical Printing Establishment" (Erhan 2000: 333). In ten years, this American mission press printed 350,000 volumes with a total of 21 million pages in Greek, Italian and Armeno-Turkish. The subjects included the lives of the prophets or apostles and reflected the life and culture of New England (Devrim 2014: 26). The *American Mission* Press moved from Malta to İzmir in 1833, and Izmir became the first center of the Western Asia Mission. In 1834, the press moved from İzmir to Istanbul and it became the center of the mission in Turkey. After serving in Pera for 20 years the printing house was named the *Bible House* (Kocabasoglu 1988). This printing press also supported the American missionary schools by providing "text books for the curriculum in Italian, the lingua franca of the Levant, and English along with vernacular languages including Turkish, Greek, Arabic, Armenian, Armeno-Turkish (Turkish written with Armenian characters), Hebrew, and Kurdish" (Devrim 2014: 27). After the Crimean war, the printing press took on a new role as a publisher of periodicals producing the Avedaper, a religious bi-monthly. Dr. Dwight was the editor of the station. The magazine became one of the press' most successful enterprises and its different editions were distributed throughout the empire. However, missionaries sometimes faced difficulties. In February 1824, some missionaries were arrested for distributing bibles, psalters and other religious books and after a couple of months their distribution was no longer allowed (The Missionary Herald 1825: 92).

Up to 1830, missionaries focused on the distribution of bibles in the languages of the native Christians. Since most Christians did not have access to the bible in their own language, the missionaries decided to focus on their translations (Kennedy 2008: 13). The ABCFM reports record that the mission press in Malta printed a total of some 350,000 copies of books and tracts (ABCFM 1834: 52). Missionaries' work in this field led to the conversion of some Muslims during the 1860s. In addition, *The Bible House* was considered one of the most successful missionary establishments in Istanbul. It was one of the most significant components within the entirety of the missionary work, as well as the official center of the American Board. It published books in Turkish for Muslims and offered the Bible in various languages. The house also published the *Missionary Herald* which was a monthly magazine through which Americans based in the Empire could read about political, economic and social events in America whilst also contributing their own experiences of Ottoman conditions via the medium of letters to the magazine. Such letters were published in the periodical, and sometimes also appeared in other American newspapers, thus providing important public information to Americans about the Ottoman Empire. Moreover, the annual report of missions, devotional books, Sunday school cards and leaflets, textbooks for all grades of schools, a weekly family newspaper, and a monthly-illustrated paper for children in three languages were also published. The Bible House also distributed the *American Board Almanac,* and delivered all of its production worldwide in India, the Ottoman Empire, Persia, Russia, and the United States (Sahin 2004: 73). However, as the missionary printing press gained recognition among Muslims, the Sublime Porte started to impose restrictions on missionary publications.

The Board's main aim, which was to reclaim the Holy Land, was re-evaluated. In the case of schools, the missionaries also realized the need for constructing missionary schools in the Empire which later became agencies of the indigenous evangelical churches. It is important to note that foreigners in the country were not allowed to purchase land and property in the Ottoman Empire before the Land Law of 1864. Prior to the introduction of this law, American missionaries, purchased land through the intermediary of a non-Muslim citizen of the Empire. The land they bought was state land and it, together with any construction that took place on the land, was registered under the nominal Ottoman subject or citizen. However, the actual owner and user of these lands and properties was the American Board. Following the enactment of the 1864 law, there was no difference between an Ottoman citizen and a citizen of a foreign country in terms of owning land and property within the Ottoman Empire, as long as the owners followed imperial laws and regulations. Moreover, as long as schools were classified as charitable establishments, they were exempted from paying taxes, fees and custom duties (Devrim 2014: 32). Missionaries also had to request the approval of the Ministry of Public Instruction for their programs of studies, text-books and for the diplomas or certificates of qualification of their teachers (Devrim 2014: 35). It is also significant to note that schools, text-books and diplomas were under the inspection of the Ministry of Public Instruction. This was a "territorial right" of the Ottoman government. In the case of the construction of American schools in Ottoman territory, this was perceived as a capitulary right of the American missionaries (Devrim 2014: 36).

On 16th November 1823, William Goodell and Isaac Bird were sent to Beirut along with their missionary wives. Upon settling in the Empire, they started to learn Turkish, Arabic and Armenian. They constructed the first American educational institutions which gave rise to reactions for two reasons. The first issue was the reaction of the local population and local authorities to the missionary establishment. The second and more important problem was the attitude of the Sublime Porte, which was basically based upon the aforementioned local reactions. The schools, as the American Board stated, would "revive knowledge and the spirit of the gospel among Oriental Churches and by this means operate upon the Muslims not to subvert them, not to proselytize, but merely re-awaken them to new duties in Christ" (The Missionary Herald 1834: 410). After the British Consulate closed down, because of the outbreak of the 1828–1829 Ottoman-Russian War, some of the American missionaries had to move to Malta (Kocabasoglu 2000: 29). Missionaries continued to establish schools in the centers of Istanbul, Beirut and Jerusalem, but they did not have any significant impact on the country until the middle of the nineteenth century. The Board itself, in 1820, stated that the schools were not considered practical as they were not sufficiently developed. Before missionary schools were established, Ottoman schools offered "reading, calligraphy and recitation." Started in the late eighteenth and early nineteenth century, the administration of schools was given to the "millets" rather than local authorities.

On 24th November 1828, the American Board assigned Rufus Anderson to make an inquiry in the Empire. In the same year the Board assigned Eli Smith and H.G.D. Dwight to make an inquiry into Anatolia, Armenia and Northwestern Iran. In sixteen months, they covered 3,000 miles. They published their observations in a report entitled *Missionary Researches in Armenia*. The report determined the Board's policies with regard to

Armenians. In January 1829 Rufus Anderson, who came to Malta, said that there was a need for the construction of more missions in Anatolia. The Prudential Committee approved the decisions that were taken in Malta and assigned Goodell to establish the necessary institutions (Kocabasoglu 2000: 30). From 1830 onwards missionary groups were sent out to explore Anatolia. Especially after the imperial edict of 1839, missionaries spread their work over many places in Anatolia. They constructed schools, printing presses, orphanages and hospitals (Baytop 2003).

The report also initiated a new mission to spread Protestantism among Syrian Armenians. In 1845, there were 34 American missionaries, 12 local officials, and 135 students in 7 schools in the Ottoman Empire. In the 1850s, American missionary schools increased their number, especially in the eastern and south-eastern regions of the country. In the 1860s, the American missionaries started the building of high schools and colleges in all the urban centers of the Ottoman territory. After the colleges were opened, more Ottoman students, mostly non-Muslim, attended these facilities and, therefore, more estates owned by Ottoman subjects were actually under the control of American missionaries. For example, the first college established by the Americans was opened in Beirut in 1866 under the name of Syria Protestant College. The missionaries were warned not to establish schools in the mountainous areas. The Ottoman government stated that it would try to protect missionaries from assaults by locals because of their educational efforts. However, it further stated that the Porte had no obligation to protect Americans who, without an imperial permit, attempted to build schools (Erhan 2000: 326). Missionaries encountered "native hostility, government oppression, famine, and banditry, political turmoil, wars, clerical opposition, local disturbances, epidemics, plagues" (Kennedy 2008: 14).

When the Protestant church became more widespread, the missionaries sought to be more self-sufficient (Kennedy 2008: 31). This led to the construction of American institutions of higher learning in the Ottoman Empire, which were initially mainly attended by non-Muslim students (Erhan 2000: 327).

One of these was Robert College, founded in Istanbul in 1863 as an extension of Bebek Seminary, and studied in more detail later in this work. During the period between 1871–1903, seven more American Colleges were opened: American Girls' College in Istanbul; Euphrates College in Harpoot; American College in Van; Central Turkey College in Marash; St. Paul's College in Tarsus; Anatolian College in Marsovan; International College in Izmir (Smyrna) (Erhan 2000: 329). Students who enrolled at these colleges were mainly Armenians, Greeks and Bulgarians. For example, the graduates of the Anatolia College in Merzifon between the years 1880–1919 almost entirely consisted of non-Muslim Armenian and Greek students (Yücel 2012: 55).

With the outbreak of the US Civil War, the American missionaries became more frugal with their funds. The missionaries were warned not to establish more stations and be careful with their distribution of funds in the country. Another solution was found as some of the missionaries either returned to the United States or simply resigned from their jobs. Missionaries in Istanbul stated that: "We have taken measures to reduce materially the expenses of the seminary and the boarding school and of our native agency - making some of these changes, indeed, not on account of pecuniary pressure, but on general principles of economy and missionary policy, and some of us have voluntarily reduced our salaries, $25, $50, or $100, hardly knowing what retrenchment can be made in family expenses, to meet this reduction" (Sahin 2004: 67). After the Civil War was over the American missionaries continued their work. However, the death of some missionaries in the war affected the station in Istanbul since the work represented individual effort.

4.1 Missionary stations and regions

Missionary stations were autonomous institutions as long as they followed the American Board's rules and instructions. Each mission set their own local regulations and protocols. At the same time, missions were divided into sub-stations. A station can be defined as an institution which is regulated under a missionary and located at the centre of a city. Under this system, there were also sub-stations or out-stations which operated on orders from the main station. Local Christians also participated in the missionary work (Kocabasoglu 2000: 69) Missionary stations were opened in Asian and European Turkey, with stations in Trabzon (1835), Erzurum (1839), Aintab (1849), Marash (1855), Adana, Aleppo, Tarsus, Hadjin,

Alexandretta, Kilis, Salonica (1850) and Izmir (1859) being constructed (Barton 1908, in Erhan 2000: 326).

Missionaries used the terms Asiatic and European Turkey in order to facilitate the locations of missionary stations in Turkey. European Turkey was used to refer to the European territories of the Ottoman Empire which included the Balkans and Thrace. In the case of Asiatic Turkey, it was further divided into three areas: Western, Central and Eastern Turkey. The Western Turkey mission covered the largest area of any mission in the Empire, which extended from Istanbul in the west to Trabzon in the eastern Black Sea region and from Smyrna on the Aegean coast to Sivas in the east. It also included a great portion of Thrace and had 102 out-stations. Even though the missionaries first disembarked at Izmir, they established the first missionary station in Istanbul. In 1860, there were 51 American missionaries and 55 native Christian missionaries; by the 1880s there were seven stations, ninety-four out-stations, twenty-one native pastors and twenty-four native preachers, 110 schools including eight girls' boarding schools and twenty-nine churches. At the same time, in the case of the press, it had produced some 347 million pages from the beginning of the mission. In 1909 the number of American missionaries had reached 85 with native Christian equivalents being recorded as 400. Missions were established with particular regard to health services in Istanbul, Marsovan, Kayseri and Sivas. Changes also took place in the missionary stations. For example, at one point the Izmir station was closed down and merged with the station in Manisa, but after 1880 the Izmir station reopened. In 1900, Istanbul and Marsovan stations became the leading stations in the Western Mission (Kocabasoglu 2000: 110).

The Central Turkey Mission, whose former name was the Southern Armenia Mission, included the cities of Adana, Tarsus and Mersin in the west of its region, and Urfa, Antep (*Aintab*) and Halep (*Aleppo*) in the east. It was the most crowded of all the missions operating health, education and printing services. For example, in 1855, Aintab had a church which had 141 members. At that time, there were more Protestants in Aintab than in Constantinople. In 1880, the mission had two stations, forty out-stations, sixty schools, including two girls' schools and Central Turkey College, and thirty-two churches. In Aintab, Dr. Azariah Smith and Rev. Benjamin Schneider were significant figures. Native evangelicals there worked hard and tried to spread the gospel in the more remote regions and even when they were trading (Stone 2006: 197). The Eastern Turkey Mission, which had previously been called the North Armenia Mission, included Erzurum in the north, Harput in the west, Van and Bitlis in the east, and Diyarbekir and Mardin in the south. The centre of this mission was Harput. (Stone 2006: 197). In 1880, the mission had 122 out-stations, twenty-three native pastors and thirty-two native preachers, 155 schools including six girls' schools, and thirty-three churches. In 1900, there were 97 edge stations in this mission. In 1859, when the seminary in Harpoot produced graduates, local people also started to participate in the mission. In 1860, the number of Americans was twenty-four which by 1914 had increased to forty-four. In the case of native workers, their number increased from 55 to 350 over the same period. Moreover, in 1857 this Armenia mission was divided into northern and southern Armenia (Devrim 2014: 29). In 1860, a church was constructed which had thirty-six members (Strong 1910: 200).

In 1856, the European Turkey mission was begun due to Dr. Hamlin's efforts. In order to increase his power, during a visit to Britain, he appealed to the Earl of Shaftesbury and the Turkish Missions' Aid Society to contribute to his work. He stated that there were four million Muslims, as well as several Christian denominations, to whom the Gospel should be spread. In the Balkans, the Bulgarians were considered to be one of the most prolific ethnic groups in the region. The Methodist Episcopal Church of North America joined the Board to work in the Balkans and assigned Rev. and Mrs. C.F. Morse, Rev. and Mrs. T.L. Byington, the Meriams, Clarks and Haskells to Adrianople (now Edirne) which is a border city. Dr. Byington would go on to become one of the most significant pioneers in Bulgaria. So that they could interact with Muslims, the missionaries were given the task of learning Turkish. The missionaries stated that people were not eager to learn about the scriptures. They would rather just keep the books (Strong 1910: 212). The mission was given $10,500 by the Society in 1860 (Shelton 2011: 219). In 1880, the mission had four stations, fifteen out-stations, three native pastors and seven native preachers, fifteen schools including two girls' schools and three churches (Washburn 2013: 111).

In 1860, debates occurred in Istanbul between the missionaries and the growing Protestant community, especially the Armenian community, on how to control funds the American Board sent for the Istanbul station.

Armenians stated that they should have a share of the money as they shared the same faith. However, the missionaries said that only the Board in Boston itself, and only the members of the American Board in Istanbul, could decide on financial matters relating to religious and administrative affairs (Sahin 2004: 66). In the same year, Dr. Dwight made a second tour around Turkey. He visited the same places as he had done on his first journey in 1830, and on both journeys made interesting observations. In 1830, he realized that the telegraph and post-roads were important tools that could assist missionary work. However, at the same time he did not find a substantial interest for his religious mission from the public. On his second trip he highlighted how improved the stations had become. For example, with regard to Marash, he said: "This place is indeed a missionary wonder" (Strong 1910: 254).

Despite the imperial decrees of 1839 and 1856, it should be borne in mind that religious persecution continued in the Ottoman Empire. In 1840 Mr. Jackson writes in the *Missionary Herald*, "The storm of persecution which has been raging in Constantinople, has put the air in motion as far off as Trebizond and Erzeroom. On the Sabbath before I left Erzeroom, a letter was read in the Armenian Church there, from the patriarchate, warning the people against the Americans, and forbidding them to patronize any schools we might open, or to purchase any of our books, and ordering them to burn them wherever found. Here in Trebizond I have not heard of precisely such orders, but the people have from the first been greatly afraid, especially those who were before somewhat friendly to us. And now we have less intercourse with them than before." (The Missionary Herald 1840, in Shelton 2011: 211). In another instance, a group of Armenians prevented a Protestant burial in Constantinople. In 1847, the Armenian Church, with the support of Jesuits, tried to force Protestant converts to change their faith. Rev. Henry van Lennep states people's names were announced and they were threatened. Some women left their husbands, or children sent their infirm parents away. Moreover, some people were physically attacked or imprisoned (Shelton 2011: 213).

In 1861, two Protestant missionaries were expelled from Hadjin. Furthermore, Mr. Coffing, an American missionary, and his Armenian companions, were shot while they were going to an annual meeting of the mission. In Mardin, Protestants faced oppression from Roman Catholics and Gregorian ecclesiastics. In 1865, two Christian converts were forced to join the army. In 1864, it was noted that the Porte violated the edict by closing book stores and imprisoning persons in order to stop the advancement of Christianity (Strong 1910: 215). In 1872, the missionary Schneiders who resided in Broosa had their house attacked and windows were broken. Another missionary, Mr. Baldwin, was also assaulted. In 1873, missionaries had to endure drought, famine and cold winter. They were also taxed for some relief and most of their stations were blocked. However, despite the hardships, they continued to carry out their work. For example, in 1877, "the Sebastopol of the Armenian Church," was opened in Van and an Evangelical society was established in the area. In Diarbekir, a split within a church was prevented with the help of Harpoot missionaries. In the case of the Western Mission, Dr. West became one of the most significant missionaries whose work reached to Sivas.

Missionary activities in Istanbul weakened in the 1870s when various missionaries were dispersed to other missions. The Board then assigned more missionaries to Istanbul, transferred Theodore A. Baldwin to the Izmir station, George F. Herrick went back to Marsovan and Henry Schauffler, the son of William G. Schauffler, to Phillippolis. Missionaries always included the Bible in their school curriculum, and made a point of becoming acquainted with the parents of their students, as well as their neighbors. In 1894, there were seventy-five men and women attending Sunday school; in 1895 the number was twice that (Sahin 2004: 87). The American Board continued its activities alone until 1870. After that year, it started to collaborate with the Board of Foreign Missions of the Presbyterian Church (BFMPC). Another organization that worked alongside the ABCFM was the Woman's Board of Missions and Woman's Board of Missions of the Interior, who were carrying out activities focused upon women and girl's education. For example, in 1912 these two institutions were supporting sixteen girls' schools with a total of 3,960 students (Kocabasoglu 2000: 96).

In the late nineteenth century, the opening of higher education institutions gained speed. Dr. Wheeler who was assigned to Harpoot amassed $50,000 from his own and his wife's savings, and opened a college in 1878. This college was first named Armenia College with its name later being changed to Euphrates College. Following its establishment, it was supported by the trustees in Massachusetts. In the same year, the Central

Turkey College in Aintab also received permission to open with student enrolment beginning in 1880. It had a varied group of students ranging from Protestants, Gregorians, Moslems, Roman Catholics to Jews (Strong 1910: 224).

Between 1876–1909, dramatic political and social events such as European intervention, irreconcilable ethnic and religious differences together with territorial disintegration affected the work of the missionaries. This period also witnessed the ascension of Sultan Abdulhamit II who established a strong autocracy and firm oversight of state and social affairs. At this time the American missionaries and their institutions were seen as threats to the traditional foundations of society, and American missionaries were under surveillance by the government. With regard to the case of missionary establishments, Sultan Abdulhamit II neither deported American missionaries nor prohibited access to their institutions. Instead, he aimed at developing Ottoman public schools as opposed to missionary schools (Devrim 2014: 33). By the late nineteenth century, the missionaries in Istanbul also demonstrated their success. For example, the missionaries gave Bible lessons in the Greek language and it was noted that more than 30 Greeks from Galata and Pera attended those sessions. In addition, theological debates also took place between Muslims and Christians and Ali Efendi, who was a Turkish Imam, participated in a Turkish service one Sunday that took place in the Bible House (Sahin 2004: 80).

By the end of the nineteenth century, the American Board had 127 Protestant congregations, 13,000 church members, 400 schools and 23,000 students (Warneck 1901, in Taskin 2007: 37). Another source states that in 1870 the American Board had 73 churches and Protestant church members exceeded 20,000. In 1900, the number of churches reached 112 and the total size of congregations reached 49,959 (Turan 1999, in Taskin 2007: 37).

In the early twentieth century, the USA and the Ottoman Empire initiated policies with regard to the ownership of American missionary establishments in Ottoman territory. American missionary schools which were associated with American missionaries requested that name changes be allowed to take place in the matter of records of property ownership. They wanted those institutions to be owned by the American Board rather than the non-Muslim intermediaries. In 1904 President Gates said that the

Robert College property of twenty-two acres was an American property protected by the American flag and Constitution (Gates 1940).

In 1904, there were 187 missionaries, 1,507 local officials and in 465 schools there were 22,867 students. As missionary schools increased their numbers, Ottoman officials applied new taxes on buildings, properties, and imported materials. Ottoman officials imposed their taxes on the buildings of colleges whether these establishments received tuition fees or not. If schools were in receipt of tuition fees, they were asked to pay half of the property taxes. If they did not receive tuition fees they were not required to pay. However, schools were required to pay tax if they moved their educational activities to larger premises. They needed to pay a sum equal to ten times thirty-percent of the current value of the new property. With regard to the import of materials from outside of Turkey, the colleges paid construction levies and custom tariffs. When the American missionaries demanded the change in ownership, the school authorities were first asked to sign a new document in order to regulate a new set of tax requirements. This document was then sent to the American Embassy for further approval from related authorities. Another obstacle Ottoman officials implemented to stop the increase of American schools, was a limitation on the size of buildings allowed to be constructed on any given piece of land. It must be noted that this size limitation not only applied to schools, but also included churches, hospitals, orphanages and other missionary institutions (Devrim 2014: 39).

The second constitutional era of the Ottoman Empire brought about a significant change in the work of the American missionaries. The group known as the Young Turks, largely composed of journalists and intellectuals, sought freedom of the press, a limitation to the Sultan's powers and, in some instances, a parliamentary government. It has been suggested that they were influenced by ideals spread by the American missionaries. George Washburn stated that "… a few young Turks first woke up to a sense of their ignorance and the need of education. They founded a society and started a periodical to promote the progress of knowledge among their people. They used to come to the American missionaries for aid and counsel. It was a new thing for the Turks, and the feeble beginning of the movement which has revolutionized the government" (Washburn 1909: 17–18). They carried out a revolution on 23rd July, 1908 taking power from Sultan Abdul Hamid II and reinstating the Constitution of 1876. Some missionaries said that they felt the Ottoman authorities adopted a more positive attitude towards them after this revolution. John G. Leishman, who was an American ambassador in Istanbul 1901–1909, stated that constitutional government not only led to the development of Ottoman society, but also brought about relief for American citizens as well as missionaries (National Archives and Records Administration, in Erhan 2000: 336) For example, in September 1908, the limited printing and distribution of books as well as restrictions on missionaries were abolished. Missionaries in the eastern part of the Empire, renovated their schools and constructed new ones. In 1913, the number of schools in the empire reached 209, and the number of pupils enrolling in those schools reached 25,922. However, the opinion of the missionaries soon started to change with the tightening of controls over missionary work, especially in the fields of schools and taxation. In 1910, the number of American kindergarten and elementary schools reached 395, housing a total of 19,243. The number of high schools reached 29, with 3,012 students enrolled in total. There were also 6 colleges and they had 1,219 students (Erhan 2000: 329).

With the outbreak of World War I, the Ottoman Empire re-shaped its policies and missionaries encountered economic problems. Capitulations were abolished, the Ottoman Empire increased its sovereign power and diplomatic relations between the United States and the Ottoman Empire were broken off in 1917 (Yücel 2012: 55). The missionaries found their activities were further limited by a combination of imperial decrees and the circumstances of the War. In 1918, the American missionaries' work came to a halt. The hospitals of the Board in Harput, Talas, Antep and Konya had been taken over by military officials in order to treat the sick and wounded soldiers (Yücel 2012: 56). Moreover, the Board had fewer staff compared to pre-war years, as the staff had decreased to 120 as compared to 168 prior to the war. In addition, among seventeen stations seven were permanently closed at the end of the war. The Board also recorded that the native work force had decreased to 324 from 1204 in 1914 (Yücel 2012: 56). With the foundation of the Turkish Republic in 1923 a new chapter began.

5 Robert College

After the Crimean War in 1856, the Ottoman Empire realized that as its power declined, education was crucial as a vehicle that could transform its government. The Empire also saw the necessity for reform in education and approved of the educational standards offered by the Americans. George Washburn states that their missionary stations, schools and colleges not only improved their students but also showed the importance of education and also introduced them to the progress of Christian civilization. Following the issue of the Imperial Edicts, missionaries were able to increase their activities as the decrees provided more liberty for Ottoman subjects. The Young Turk Revolution also led to the Ottoman Empire adopting western ideals such as liberty, justice, equality and fraternity for all races and religions of the Empire. Robert College is considered as a significant American institution which symbolizes the impressive achievement of American educational enterprise. It became one of the leading places of learning in the region and a model for later missionary schools. Some people suggest that Robert College became perhaps the best institution after the "Bible House at Constantinople" that American missionaries ever established (Hamlin 1893). One of the reasons for the success of the College would seem to be its aim of promoting the physical, intellectual and moral aspects of its students. This is consistently evidenced via the College's curriculum. From the start, students had to produce intensive coursework that led to significant progress. The College campus had a library and a museum, which are further proof that the College's education was designed to reflect the highest standards of that time and be recognized internationally. Robert College's students, whether graduates or even dropouts, have attained the highest roles in their societies, and these successes have ensured that Robert College alumni are willing to enrol their offspring in the same school, thus guaranteeing the College's future and enhancing its reputation even further. Another significant objective of education at the College was the teaching of freedom. The college aimed to teach its students the real meaning of freedom and the responsibility that individual freedom requires. In order to do so, it offered more freedom to its students at a younger age. The students learned by doing how to use their individual freedom and the responsibilities that came with that freedom. The college's education was based upon a humanistic approach which supported the idea that education trains and improves people's moral values, capabilities and character. In other words, people's character can be shaped through education. It is important to emphasize that Robert College was first of all a Christian missionary school which, due to the inclusion of religious education within its curriculum, had the support of high ranking clergy within the eastern churches. Because of its educational success Robert College became known not only in the Ottoman Empire, but also in Europe, as a successful institution that represented the United States and spread its ideals in the east. The college gained recognition from Europe, Ottoman Empire, Iran and Russia and even south-eastern European countries. In the beginning, the college was established with a small amount of money, and it faced financial difficulties from time to time. However, the college has managed to maintain its presence to today due to the faith, sacrifice and devotion of its pioneers. The college owes its continued success to its educational policies, teaching methods, curriculum, teachers and administrative staff and by accepting talented and intelligent students. The College has always held to the belief that the most advanced moral development can be obtained through physical, intellectual and religious teaching. Religious education was not specific to any one particular faith, but it was practical teaching based upon the fact that all people have freedom of conscience. According to this principle and the college's establishment aim, the students were expected to attend morning prayers and church services on Sunday. On the weekdays, every morning class started with morning prayers, on the weekends boarding students attended morning and evening prayers. However, this rigid application of Christianity varied somewhat according to the attitudes of the College leadership, as will be addressed later in this work. When the Turkish Republic was founded, religious services in the college were abolished and Bible class was only taught to Christian students (Acun and Gürata 2016: 3).

5.1 The Construction of Robert College

Cyrus Hamlin was the one of the most important educational representatives of the American Board in Istanbul. He was an educator, inventor, technician, architect, builder who established a school for boys in Bebek in which there were 15 students during its first year of operation. The number doubled in the next year (Anderson 1872: 122–3). Later this school was turned into a seminary. The courses included theology, academic subjects and language instruction. Cyrus Hamlin was also known for his bakery and his work to support the military hospital in Scutari, for which he helped with the construction of a laundry for military officials in order to help them wash their clothes and thus raise standards of hygiene. In so doing he was able to gain the confidence of both military officials and the local people. After the Crimean War, he was able to assemble a fund of $25,000 which he contributed to the construction of thirteen churches that helped the development of Protestantism among Armenians. His seminary was also supported by local people. It drew students not only from Constantinople, but also from remote areas of the empire. For example, in 1852 two students came from Diyarbekir, with both of them eventually going on to become pastors of young churches located at Harpoot and Diyarbakir. More than 100 students were registered in the seminary with Armenian, Greek and English being the major languages that were spoken there (Strong 1910: 199). Later Cyrus Hamlin demanded that the American Board's Executive Committee in Boston extend the scope of missions by establishing a high-quality English medium college. However, Rufus Anderson, the Secretary of the Board, did not appreciate the idea because he thought the Bebek Seminary, and the missionaries in Istanbul in general, should keep preparing students to be pastors rather than offering education in English per se. In 1856, Christopher Rheinlander Robert, a rich business man, merchant and philantrophist from New York City, came to Istanbul on a visit. He was impressed by the missionary work in Istanbul. In the same year, ABCFM announced that the only work of the missionary was to "preach the Gospel in public or private" (Washburn 2013: 1). Mr. Robert realized that this could best be accomplished by constructing a school. Then, the idea of constructing a college in Constantinople was suggested to Mr. Robert in 1857 by Messrs. James and William Dwight. They suggested that the college would gain the support of people in Istanbul and it would grow out of the Bebek Seminary. Christopher Robert stated that he would donate twenty to thirty thousand dollars on condition that he would not be identified and remain anonymous, and Cyrus Hamlin would be the administrator of the institution.

Cyrus Hamlin, in his book *Among the Turks,* states that with Mr. Robert he established Christian college that shall offer the best intellectual training (Hamlin 1877, in Freely 2000: 53). Thus, the Board approved the opening of Robert College. The school was under a charter granted by the Legislature of New York and appointed Cyrus Hamlin as its first director. Hamlin had to resign from his position with the American Board in order to join the college in the Ottoman Empire. Clearly the college was named after the after the donor Christopher Robert and it became Robert College. Christopher Robert's gifts to the school, including the designated gift in his will, totalled at least $600,000 (Shelton 2011: 59). At the time when the college was being constructed, the Board was opposed to spending money on education. It is important to note that when Dr. Hamlin went to the USA to raise funds for the school in 1860, the US was on the verge of civil war. However, Hamlin and his colleagues were determined to accomplish their project.

The Sublime Porte did not initially want to allow the College's opening because it was to be a comprehensive foreign educational institution. Russian and French influence also acted upon the Sublime Porte's approach. With Robert College being established, it was expected that there could be a conflict between the Ottoman Government and other western countries. Moreover, the Sublime Porte was concerned about western ideals such as "liberalism" and "nationalism" being imposed on Ottoman subjects including Bulgarians, Armenians and Albanians which could have "destructive" reflections on the Empire (Erhan 2000: 13). For example, it was believed that Robert College caused the loss of Bulgaria during the early twentieth century because it educated and supported individual freedom among the Bulgarians (Kirsehirlioglugil 1963).

In addition, the location of Robert College also led to disputes. The Sublime Porte was not in favor of constructing a school in Rumeli Hisari as the area was mostly occupied by Muslims. Dr. Hamlin continued negotiations for the site for nearly seven years. Most of the existing non-Muslim schools were located in the areas of Pera, Fener and St. Stephanos because these were the places where non-Muslims lived. Thus, the Sublime Porte sought to contain the churches, missionary stations and schools within those areas (Kerner 1948: 160–71). After the Rumeli Hisar site was finally purchased, in March 1862 the Minister of Foreign Affairs acknowledged to the English ambassador and the American minister that they were allowed to build the college. In 1871, Robert College moved to a bigger building on the same site.

The college was named after its benefactor Christopher Robert, despite his objections. Cyrus Hamlin stated that the name would be more suitable for a multi-ethnic audience in which several languages are spoken. For example, "American College" was deemed unacceptable as it was "too tainted with democracy." Another name proposed was "The College of Constantinople" but this was not accepted either since it sounded "too assuming". Yet another suggestion was "The Oriental College" which was not found suitable by some because it was plainly untrue. In the case of Robert College it fitted with many languages and would not offend anyone (Freely 2000: 61). In regard to sanctions by the Ministry of Public Instruction, Cyrus Hamlin stated: "… the college would be conducted in loyalty to the Turkish government, and in accordance with the character of American colleges, which have no political or partisan character. Our library, our textbooks and all college exercises would be open to inspection every day from morning prayers, in which the Sultan and his empire would be prayed for, until 9 o'clock in the evening" (Hamlin 1889: 198).

In order not to be sanctioned by the American Board, the administration of the college adopted a self-support policy which was based on continuous fund raising. As George Washburn was engaged in the search for funds, he wrote that Robert College "has acquired a worldwide reputation as a model American Christian College… The people of the East have manifested their confidence… [and] all the Christian churches of the East are in sympathy with it… the Trustees earnestly appeal to friends of the College, and to all those who benefit in the power of a Christian education or who care for American influence in Europe and the East, for funds" (Sahin 2004: 23).

5.2 Education at Robert College

Moral values, religion and languages played key roles at Robert College. The College's teaching focused on improving human values, abilities and character, with much effort being spent on training students in moral and religious values as well as forms of politeness and good attitude. The main principle of the college was to teach students the curriculum subjects (in English) and how to express themselves in the best way possible. Apart from that the students were expected to learn and improve their good manners. In Robert College it was believed that schools and family were the institutions within which improvement of good manners and etiquette can be learned. It was not possible for these to be learned in the society as a whole. In this sense, the College must lead its students. With social activities such as balls, receptions, concerts and picnics, the students learned: how to behave in public; how to behave when they met somebody new; how to behave when they accompanied a lady; or at a formal evening dinner; or when they attended a concert. Such lessons were mandatory in most European colleges. Robert College believed someone's inner beauty and honesty can only be seen through their external actions and the latter can be moderated via education. Apart from these social activities, rules on how students should behave were formulated and hung on various walls and doors throughout the college (Acun and Öztunca 2016: 5–7).

Even though, the college's education system was designed to be parallel with the principles of the Bible and to be administrated accordingly, with the College's constitution proclaiming that religious classes would take place with the participation of all students, the College's education system was actually formed according to Cyrus Hamlin's views and ideals (Greenwood 2000: 16). Schools like Robert College were not only good Christian institutions reflecting the appropriate religious ideals, but the curriculum also included secular elements. In fact, Hamlin's views often conflicted with those of the Board. The Board emphasized training native Protestant preachers, while Hamlin took a broader approach and aimed at training people who would contribute to the modernization process that was taking place in the Ottoman Empire. Therefore, Hamlin arranged a curriculum that would concentrate on English and Science classes. However, most of the Board's members believed that such an education would instill secular ideas and would lead students to be seekers of earthly material benefits. In addition, students would not be eager to make sacrifices and would rather live in the capital or big cities instead of devoting their lives to the mission that could take place in the remote corners of Anatolia (Greenwood 2000, in Acun and Öztunca 2016: 4).

In the case of the school's stance on religion, Mr. Dwight suggested that the school should be secular. However, according to Mr. Robert and supporters of the school, it should represent a Christian faith. Dr. Hamlin stated that it must be "a decided, thorough Christian school from its very commencement or it would not secure the confidence of the people" (Washburn 2013: 4). Thus the constitution of the school laid down that the school would be "un-sectarian and open to all without distinction of race or Christian churches of the East." The school did not aim to make propaganda against other Christian faiths, but it sought to improve the spiritual life of its students. The school was supported by major American universities such as Harvard (Washburn 2013: 8). The constitution further stated that "it is to be founded and administered on the principles of the Bible: it is hereby declared and ordained that, while it is to be a scientific and literary institution, God and His word shall be distinctly acknowledged and honored therein: the Scriptures, as published by the American or British and Foreign Bible Societies being read and prayers offered at least once each day of each collegiate term, and Divine worship held on the Sabbath, at which services the Faculty are expected to be present, and all the students shall attend unless for special and imperative reasons some are excused by the Faculty and teachers" (Washburn 2013: 14–15). In the college, students were not taught about their own religious beliefs, but only received religious education on the Protestant faith and attended Protestant church services. Religious education was only based upon the Bible and it was mandatory for students to go to morning prayers every day; to attend Sunday Prayers; to take part in Bible readings in the afternoon; to attend religious and new year's celebrations; to be part of Young Men's Christian Association's activities and to be present for religious gatherings every night. Between 1903–1932, Dr. Gates, who was the head of Robert College, arranged the College's educational program and decided to open an Engineering School to further meet the needs of a liberal education based on technical instruction in the English language. The liberal atmosphere brought about by the Second Constitutional Era together with the needs of the Empire also supported this development (Greenwood 2000).

The theology seminars that were offered in the college were in line with the evangelistic ideas of the American Board. One of the College's objectives was to train students as future preachers and ministers to disseminate the Protestant gospel in their Ottoman homelands, without migrating back to the United States (Devrim 2014: 34). There were differing views as to whether students should attend religious services. Rev. Schauffler and Perkins believed that the College was part of the broader evangelical mission. Thus, students must attend the services. Cyrus Hamlin, on the other hand, took more a liberal stance on the issue. He stated that it was true that the college was Christian in character. However, this did not mean that the services should be mandatory. For example, he would allow his students to attend their own religion's services or he could excuse them for not attending any service whatsoever. In 1864, both Schauffler and Perkins resigned from their positions. Cyrus Hamlin defended himself as he wrote to Mr. Robert about this matter. He stated that both Schauffler and Perkins were neglecting their duties and were criticizing everything he had done. He went on to suggest that maybe he should be the one who resigned from his job. Both Schauffler's and Perkins' resignations were accepted (Freely 2000: 63). After Perkins' and Schauffler's departure, Hamlin's son-in-law, George Washburn, took their positions. He had obtained a degree in divinity at the Andover Theological Seminary and had been ordained a minister. Dr. Hamlin stated that the school improved in a steady fashion and they did not encounter difficulties neither during religious services nor the teaching of the Bible in classes (Washburn 2013: 20). In the case of George Washburn, he believed that religious instruction should be mandatory, irrespective of the students' church affiliation. In 1873, in his letter to Christopher Robert, he wrote: "I fully approve of your suggestion in regard to the Ten Commandments and they will be read every Sabbath except when Dr. Hamlin takes charge. He does not quite fancy this idea…" (Freely 2000: 97).

The school's language of instruction was English. It was chosen because it was a common language that would enable communication among different "races" and "tongues". In addition, the wide availability of textbooks in English was another reason why English became the language of instruction. The ABCFM suggested that the courses in the college should be taught in the native language and the number of native teachers and American teachers should be the same. However, Cyrus Hamlin opposed this idea and said that in order to liberate Ottoman subjects from their previous teaching, the school should adopt "the principles of New England religious tradition" such as egalitarianism, progressivism, as well as pursuit of individual salvation and intellectual formation, American analytical and inquisitive research and teaching methods and Protestant Christian values. Apart from English, every student was expected to learn another western language. In addition, the students were required to learn Latin and speak their own language at an advanced level. Thus, the number of languages that students were required to learn was four. Teaching of old and modern languages at an advanced level was one of the most significant features of Robert College.

In 1863, Mr. Robert emphasized that the school must ensure it gave a thorough education. He wrote to Cyrus Hamlin "I note there was a tremendous pressure on you to make it a "mere school of Languages." This must be resisted at all hazards, for my design is to establish an institution in which a thorough scientific education can be obtained to be as equal as soon as practicable to that given by Yale or any other first class college in this country…it conforms to my idea that ultimately the college will grow into a university with departments for the study of theology and law" (Freely 2000: 97).

5.3 Requirements for tutors in Robert College as of 1868

The candidate should be a male. His age should range from twenty-two to twenty-six. He should show a strong missionary spirit. He must be hardworking and willing to cooperate with others. He must be perseverant and should follow the college's rules. He should live a good Christian life and be a good Christian teacher. He should show his desire for helping his students and he must try to improve their understanding. The tutor should have a strong mind. He should have a share of common sense, a firm but mild temper, a warm heart so that he can construct strong relationships with others. He must be perceptive and unbiased. He should be able to govern himself as well as others. He should have a broad understanding of education. He must be a thorough and systematic scholar, not just a man who graduated from college. He must be a real enthusiast in learning and must always seek to improve himself. He should demonstrate that he understands the essence of education. He must have aptitude to teach and he should be able to demonstrate what he knows. He must work enthusiastically and should be determined to make his students better scholars. He should be able to impress his students. His words should be considered as law to his students. He must be punctual and prompt. The tutor should not work for the sake of money (Freely 2000: 67–8).

5.4 Enrolment in the College

Application to the college was made by means of a letter written by the parent of the student. The academic year started in the fall semester in September. Students who were transferring from other schools were required to bring their academic transcripts, and new students who enrolled had to provide reports on their social, health and mental conditions. They were further required to bring a certificate which showed that they had been vaccinated within the past four years. If they had not been vaccinated, the College's doctor vaccinated them and they were required to pay a fee. Students who came from outside the Ottoman Empire had to have a guardian who resided in Istanbul, and all correspondence was carried out via this person (Acun and Gürtunca 2016: 8). Those wishing to enrol in the College's Preparatory Department, should have good knowledge their own native tongue and were expected to solve basic arithmetic problems using the four operations. Prep School lasted two or three years, depending on the performance of the individual student. In this time eighteen subjects were taught divided into language learning, social science and arithmetic (Acun and Gürtunca 2016: 8).

5.5 Preparatory School

The Prep School was considered to be the first step in the College's education. As stated above, the program's duration was two or three years. Today the duration of a Robert College education is five years: one year Preparatory School and four years high school. In 1920, the Prep School's name was changed to Robert Academy and its duration became six years. The fifth and sixth years of the program were called "sub-freshman" and became the most significant pre-requisite for the transition to the College itself. The large, fire-proofed Theodorous Hall was reserved for Prep School, with the Head of the School, his wife and a couple of teachers staying in that building which was close to the student dormitories. This ensured that they were able to closely supervise their students. The students were provided with adequate food and were not allowed to bring food from outside, or from their parents. In addition, the places where students could spend money were limited, thus parents were advised to give little allowance to their children (Acun and Gürtunca 2016: 8).

5.6 The College curriculum

Science: In the college science was divided into five categories: natural science, physics, chemistry, geology and mining.

Arithmetic and Geometry: Arithmetic started in the first year of Prep School and lasted till the end of the first semester of senior year. In the first year, the course was taught in vernacular language and then it was taught in English. It included geometry, trigonometry, analytic geometry, calculus and commercial arithmetic. This course lasted so long in comparison to others because it taught students mathematics from basic principles to quite advanced techniques, and also encouraged rational and abstract thinking.

History: The teaching of history started in the second year of Prep School and lasted till the end of senior year. The college not only aimed at teaching students the past, but also at shaping their identities. History subjects included Eastern nations' history, old Greek and Roman history, middle ages and contemporary times, Byzantine, European and American history. The students were also taught about the history and civilizations of countries surrounding Istanbul. While teaching history, teachers were meticulous in taking the most unbiased approach. Teaching students their own history, as well as that of their neighbours, was designed to give them a broader perspective which would lead to students becoming more tolerant and sympathetic to their surroundings.

Geography: During the first year of education, geography was taught in the vernacular language and later it was taught in English. The scope of the course included local and global geography. European, Asian, African, American and Australian geographies were taught and were divided into time periods. In this context, industrial, commercial and physical aspects of the subject were highlighted. The course book was (Acun and Gürtunca 2016: 12–17).

Literature: The course was designed to teach general literature lessons. It lasted one hour. Major English, French and Greek literary works were studied and the course included English composition and oratory (Acun and Gürtunca 2016: 18–20).

Music: Students learned to play flute, mandolin and guitar, with piano and violin as optional instruments. A student orchestra was also established and concerts were given on special days and anniversaries. In 1896, the class was taught in the first and third semesters of the second year under musical theory. In the following years, the number and duration of musical classes was increased. Between 1920 and 1930 the course was given every year in the high school section. The students also formed a choir and many professional musicians emanated from the College.

Drawing and Painting: Drawing, which later became painting, was taught during Prep School and sub-freshman year.

Parliamentary Law, International Law and Civil Government: As of 1896, parliamentary law was taught in the second year; international law was taught in the fourth year and civil government was taught in the third year of the College. Following the formation of the Republic of Turkey these classes were abolished.

Sociology: As of 1896, senior students took this course for three hours per week. According to the educational directive of 1935, it was left to the decision of college administrators whether or not to teach this course in Turkish to foreign students.

Citizenship and Civics: This course was first introduced in 1930, and was taught in Turkish to foreign students by Turkish teachers.

Anthropology: As of 1896, this subject was taught to the senior year students for one hour per week. With the coming of the Republican regime, this was another subject which was excluded from the curriculum.

Logic: As of 1896, this was taught to the junior year students for three hours within the philosophy syllabus. Another subject that ceased to be taught after 1924 when the Republican regime issued its regulations for what could, and could not, be taught.

Bible: The class was taught to Christian students. From the initial establishment of the College, the Holy Scripture and Biblical Literature classes were mandatory courses. The course was arranged by the Young Men's Christian Association. Under the 1924 regulations, religious courses and worship continued in foreign schools. However, apart from within sanctuaries/

churches/chapels, religious sculptures, portraits and representations of the cross were not allowed to be created. The directive also prohibited religious propaganda. It emphasized that school and church were different places and religious propaganda would not be tolerated. In other words, measures were taken to prevent religious propaganda not the religion itself.

Evidence of Christianity: This was taught to Christian students in the first semester of the senior year of the college until it was removed from the curriculum in 1924.

Morality: In 1896, this course was taught in the second semester of the fourth year in the College.

Behavior: This class considered students' behaviour in class and within their daily lives in college, their following of rules and their behavior towards their friends and teachers were evaluated. The course aimed at developing the personality/character of individual students as well as teaching them good manners; an early equivalent of a modern personal and social development course. This course was another one which was abolished following the creation of the Republic of Turkey. Students' behavior was also included in Department Records.

Handicraft: This was taught in 1940 at Prep School level and in 1953 during the third year in the College. It aimed to develop student hand and coordination skills via a range of crafts.

Industrial Education: This was only taught in the second and third years of College as a one hour per week class in 1930. It must be presumed that this subject was not successful or the lecturer who taught it left the College's employment (Acun and Gürtunca 2016: 18–23).

Military: This subject entered the curriculum after World War II. In 1970 it was listed as Military Science. It aimed at improving students' knowledge of security, strategy and military matters in general.

Commerce and Accounting: In 1951, first year students were taught commerce and second year students received accounting classes. These classes taught the basics of commerce and practical accounting and were designed to prepare students for the world of business. In 1912 a designated Accounting Department was opened in the College for the first time. The Department offered commercial arithmetic, accounting, finance, correspondence, law and banking and students also received typewriting courses.

Physical Training: Senior year students received physical training courses to improve their bodily capabilities, and there were also football and baseball teams in the school. An Athletic Faculty was established and basketball was introduced to Ottoman Empire for the first time. In 1920, Robert College's basketball team was founded.

Secondhand Book Trading: This was an interesting elective course available to first year students. It aimed at obtaining, preserving or selling old printed and handwritten books.

Calligraphy: In order to emphasize the importance of beautiful, yet legible, handwriting this course was taught throughout Prep School and freshman year. In 1930, it was taught for three years in high school.

Exams: In order to measure their knowledge, students took exams from every course in which they were involved on a monthly basis. Quizzes and oral exams also took place when teachers found them necessary. All written and oral exams were graded from 1–10 with the scale being as follows: 10–9 very good; 8 good; 7 satisfactory; 6 can pass; below 6 failed. The grades that students received were collated at the end of each month within a report to parents. The student was asked to have his parents to sign this report as proof that it had been received. At the end of each semester, an average of the student's monthly grades was calculated and collated with the final examination grade that s/he received giving a grade for the semester. Students who attained less than 6 from three or more classes were deemed to have failed (Acun and Gürtunca 2016: 22–3). Those who received below six from one or two classes would retake those classes within a set time period. In the case of failure in final exams at the end of a semester, students could take resit exams which were available three times each year: at the end of summer semester, New Year and Easter. In the case of College entrance exams, they were offered twice a year in June and September following the opening of a new school year (Acun and Gürtunca 2016: 23).

5.7 The historical development of the College

In the first year, the school only had four students: three English and one American. Before that academic year ended 20 people had registered for the next academic session. In the faculty there were two American professors. Firstly, Rev. George Perkins who was a graduate of both Bowdoin College and Bangor Theological Seminary. In 1853, he had become a missionary in Anatolia, then later returned to the US and studied at the Sheffield Scientific School at Yale. Finally he became a Professor of Natural Science at the College. He brought a telegraph which he had received from Samuel F.B. Morse himself.

The other American professor was Rev. Henry A. Schauffler who had graduated from Williams College in 1859 and gone on to study theology at Andover and law at Harvard. He also carried out postgraduate study at the University of Heidelberg, then he became Professor of Theology at Robert College. The other faculty members were a Greek Professor, Mr. Kazakos; a Professor of French, M. Dalem; a Professor of Italian and Design, M. Marchesi; and at a later a period a Professor of Armenian, Mr. Hagopos Gigizan; besides other teachers employed at various times for specific subjects. However, the decision board only included Hamlin, Perkins and Schauffler. Cyrus Hamlin further added that Protestants were too poor to pay the $200 tuition fee (Freely 2000: 61).

In the second year, 1864–1865, the school opened with 23 students and 28 in all were registered during the year of whom, 4 were Greeks, 1 Armenian and 1 Bulgarian. In the fifth college year, 1867–68, it opened with a full number of students. One hundred and two were registered during the year, of whom, 14 were Armenians, 16 Bulgarians, 33 Greeks. In the sixth college year, there were 80 students and 95 in all were registered during the year, of whom, 11 were Armenians, 41 Bulgarians, 17 Greeks. Both cholera and fire in Istanbul reduced the number of students who registered at the school. In the third academic year of 1865–1866, there were only eight students. At the end of the term, the number rose to fifty-one among then there were 20 Armenians, 9 Bulgarians and 6 Greeks (Freely 2000: 61).

Later, the Armenian and Bulgarian students constituted the majority then, during the first two decades of the twentieth century, Greek students outnumbered the others. In the case of Turks, they were first enrolled in the school year of 1866–1867. Following the establishment of the Republic of Turkey in 1923, it was observed that Turkish students increased their number. Moreover, the Young Turk Revolution of 1908 and the establishment of the Turkish Republican regime would seem to have had a direct impact on the number of enrolments at Robert College (Sabev 2011, 2014). In the year 1954–1955, Turks numbered 780 out of a total student body of 1051, which means they constituted 74 percent of Robert College's students (Sabev 2014: 147). The total number of the students whose nationality is stated as Turkish during the Ottoman period of Robert College is 706 (Sabev 2014: 155). For example, Kiamil Efendi and the brothers H. and E. Williams were the first Turkish students of the college. They were called "Christian Osmanlis" because they converted from Islam to Christianity (Sabev 2014: 156).

As student numbers increased Cyrus Hamlin and Christopher Robert had to hire more instructors. The new tutors were Edwin A. Grosvenor and S.D. Wilcox with John Alsop Paine being hired at the professorship level. He later took the charge of the program in natural sciences. Both Wilcox and Paine graduated from Hamilton College, with Grosvenor, being a graduate of Amherst. Paine also held an MA from Hamilton and was a graduate of Andover Theological Seminary. He had studied Botany at Harvard University and, in 1867, he had been ordained.

In the fifth year, there were two candidates for graduation. They were Hagop Cecizian and Petco Garbonoff. Both of them became teachers in the College the following year. The first commencement was held before a broad audience in which people chatted in Turkish, Armenian, Bulgarian and French, as well as English. The diplomas were issued in four languages: French, English, Turkish and Armenian or Bulgarian. In 1868–1869, the number of enrolled students reached 95. Among them there were 41 Bulgarians, 17 Greeks and 11 Armenians (Freely 2000: 62).

George Washburn joined the faculty by the end of the term. About three-fourths of the students boarded in the college, 73 in all. They studied in the study hall, slept in the dormitories, 12 or 15 together, bringing their own bedding, ate in the dining room, played in the small court, made their ablutions in a small lavatory or in the open court, got exercise by walking and occasional games on the hills above Bebec. They had prayers conducted by Dr. Hamlin at 6.30 in the morning and any student who failed to be present lost his breakfast. Each dormitory had a tutor's room next to it, and the tutors were expected to keep a surveillance over the students at all times, but especially in the study halls and the dormitories. No student could leave the building without special permission (Freely 2000: 73).

Prior to his arrival in Istanbul, George Washburn was working as a treasurer in the American Board. In the College, he started to teach and became an intermediary for land purchases. In his memoir he states that "Dr. Hamlin telephoned me to come at once, and we arrived in Constantinople in season to be present at the laying of the corner stone of the new building at Hissar, July 5, 1869, and went to live in one of the college buildings in Bebec just opposite the main building. The college was still in session" (Freely 2000: 74). Dr. Hamlin writes "We welcome the Washburns with great rejoicing, for all these difficulties so absorb my time that the college year would wind up badly without him. My official position was that of Professor of Philosophy." (Freely 2000: 74).

The year 1869 marked the seventh year of the college. In that year, two new tutors from the US were appointed. E.W. Wetmore of Michigan University and Charles Anderson of Hamilton College, and together with Mr. Grosvenor they entered into the work with enthusiasm and whole-hearted devotion. There were six assistant teachers. In the same year, there were 53 boarders and 18 scholars. Among these 71 students, there were 35 Bulgarians, 10 Greeks, 8 Armenians, 6 Americans, 4 English, 2 Dutch, 2 Syrians, 2 Christian Osmanlis, 1 Persian Prince, 1 German (Freely 2000: 88). In 1871, Bulgarians constituted most of College's population of 99 students divided into 74 boarders and 25 day scholars. In 1872, there were 150 boarders and 45 day students giving a total enrolment of 95. In May 1873 there were 215 students in total: 170 boarders and a further 45 attending on a daily basis. The number of Jews among the student body increased from year to year. The aforementioned 215 students enrolled in 1873 can be further divided into 76 studying in the Prepatory Department; 80 in the Intermediate Department; and 59 in the Collegiate Department. The Intermediate Department included students who were considered to have not yet reached a sufficient standard for admission to the Collegiate Department, and were repeating their previous year's study (Freely 2000: 80–90).

In the ninth academic year, there were 210 students enrolled in the college. In the same year, there were eight graduates, six of whom were

Bulgarians, one Greek and one English. In the tenth academic year, disputes occurred between Greek, Bulgarian and Armenian students because of their differing stances on their respective churches. In that year there were 257 students enrolled in the College: 189 boarders and 68 day scholars. From this total population only 54 went on to graduate. In fact it should be noted that since the foundation of the College, not more than one in six students has completed the course and graduated. There are several reasons why this is the case. These include the College's demanding curriculum; the fact that some students enrolled in the college merely for the cachet of having attended and left early when their parents offered them a business opportunity; for some students financial limitations were also an issue. In addition, professional life including positions in the government did not always demand the requirement of a college education (Freely 2000: 96). In addition, it should be noted that the Armenian Gregorian Church also urged its communicants to attend Robert College regardless of their future plans.

In the academic year of 1878–1879, George Washburn became the tenured President of Robert College. The year was also important as it was the year when the Treaty of Berlin was signed. Washburn first appointed Alexander van Milligen as Professor of History in the College. Van Millingen was already known for his work on topography and the monuments of Byzantine Constantinople. At the beginning of that academic year, there were 96 boarders and 38 day scholars, and in that year the first catalog of Robert College was published (Freely 2000: 96).

Robert College is also known for its role in the construction of independent Bulgaria. For example, the British journalist and historian Sir Edwin Pears states that "I know no other instance in history where a single institution has so powerfully affected the life of a nation as Robert College has affected the life of Bulgaria". Another writer, W.T. Snead, stated that "Robert College made Bulgaria". However, Cyrus Hamlin strongly opposed the idea that Robert College contributed to the independence of Bulgaria. "I am in no way responsible for the absurd stories which are current in regard to my life and influence here which appear from time to time in the newspapers. I never had any acquaintance with any Sultan. I did not make the Russo-Turkish War and I did not create Bulgaria. I never had anything to do with revolutionary plots and never encouraged the Bulgarians to rebel against the Turkish government. On the contrary I have used all my influence to discourage these revolutionary movements... Robert College has never been the centre of sedition" (Freely 2000: 122).

In the academic year of 1887, there were 26 graduates: 13 Bulgarians, 10 Armenians and 3 Greeks. Some of them went on to be government officials (4); 3 became teachers; 3 physicians; 10 merchants; 1 lawyer; 1 physician; 1 publisher; 1 civil engineer; 1 dentist. In the academic year of 1888 there were 15 Bulgarians some of whom went on to become: physicians (3); 3 worked as teachers; 2 judges; 2 merchants; 1 lawyer; 1 government official; 1 civil engineer. Among the Armenian graduates of that year 6 became merchants; 2 teachers; 2 government officials; 1 civil engineer; 1 agriculturist. In the academic year of 1889, Charles Anderson was appointed to be Professor of Ethics, Rhetoric, Oratory and Physical Culture. He had graduated from Andover Theological College and at the time of his appointment was the pastor of a church in Woburn, Massachusetts. In the same year, the construction of new buildings began. One building was constructed for the College President's residency, which is today called Kennedy Lodge. The other structure was built to contain science laboratories and classrooms. To finance the building work Mr. Washburn went to the USA to raise funds. In 1889, there were 164 students which was the same number as the previous year. Among them there were 45 Bulgarians, 47 Armenians, 41 Greeks, 20 English and Americans, 11 others. In 1892, the Science Hall was completed (Freely 2000: 120–5).

In 1893, the college was affected by earthquakes and the plague which hit Istanbul. "When the thirty-first college year was opened, Constantinople was surrounded by quarantine stations which made all travel very difficult, and at about the same time cholera broke out in the city and continued with more or less severity until April, with sanitary regulations which caused even more excitement and alarm than the disease itself. The number of students coming from Bulgaria also fell seriously" (Freely 2000: 131). The appointment of new teachers led to a decrease in the salaries of the professors. There were 13 graduates that year: 6 Bulgarians, 3 Armenians, 3 Greeks and 1 Englishman, seven of whom went on to become: merchants (2); 2 lawyers; 3 physicians. One of the Greek graduates, Stavros Emmanuel, became an instructor at Robert College with a further two Armenian graduates, Mihran Djedjizian and Tsvetan G. Ilieff, also becoming teachers in the College (Freely 2000: 131).

1894 was the first year that Greek students outnumbered Armenians and Bulgarians. Washburn also adds that Miss Stokes of New York contributed to the establishment of a new building. In the academic year of 1900–1901, Mr. Lybyer was appointed to the Mathematics department, he later became a historian. With regard to the commencement of 1901, George Washburn states: "The most interesting events at the Commencement were the Gathering of the alumni and a letter received from the Greek Patriarch. For the first time we had an alumni dinner, at which more than sixty were present, a large number considering that our alumni were scattered over the world and that the obstacles put in the way of travel prevent those from abroad coming to Constantinople" (Freely 2000: 155). In 1901–1902, Professor William S. Murray was appointed as Principal of the Preparatory Department; Dr. Charles W. Ottley as physician and Professor of Biology; Professor S. Murray as treasurer; Professor George L. Manning as Professor of Physics; the Rev. C.F. Gates D.D., LL.D. was appointed Vice President.

According to George Washburn the College's success can be observed from its alumni. They were able to go to the best universities in Europe as scholars. They were also easily recognized wherever they went as they represented a different type of manhood to that which was normally seen in the east. The college also contributed to ensuring people of different races were able to work harmoniously, as students were treated equally and thus were able to develop respect for each other. The students learned how to work together towards a common end with the college eliminating prejudices and representing the values of Christianity and the United States (Freely 2000: 159).

Robert College's third President was Caleb Frank Gates who had graduated from Beloit College in 1877 and the following year continued his studies at the Chicago Theological School. In 1881, he was assigned to missionary work in the Ottoman Empire by the ABCFM and first worked in Mardin, where his job was to distribute funds collected in the US for the relief of impoverished peasants. In 1894, he became president of Euphrates College. John S. Kennedy, who was the president of the Board of Trustees of Robert College, proposed him as the next President and, in 1903, he duly became the President of Robert College. At that time, 320 students of fourteen different nationalities were registered at the College. Among them there were a mere six Turks. Sultan Abdulhamit's discouraging policies had led to this small number of Turks being enrolled. However, Turks who did enrol were united in their praise of Robert College as it not only contributed to an improvement in their scientific knowledge, but also increased their moral character. A Turkish minister said that: "I do not know much about the instruction that Robert College gives in science and history; but one thing I know is it makes men" (Freely 2000: 163).

In the year 1907, there were more than 20 Turks registered in the college. From the American perspective, as Turks became more enlightened, their demand for higher education increased. Robert College also benefited from the political climate in the Ottoman Empire. In particular when the Young Turks (Committee of Union and Progress) carried out a military coup against Sultan Abdulhamit II, compelling him to enforce the 1876 Ottoman Constitution which was written by Midhat Pasha. With their intervention a new era started which lasted from 1908 to 1918.

George Washburn perceived this act as a sign of "Enlightenment" and certainly the revolution would seem to have had a positive affect on the number of Turks enrolling as students in the College. In the academic year of 1909–10, it was recorded that the number of Turkish students doubled compare to previous years. Looking at enrolment numbers over the whole life of the College to 1922 we see: "the average number of Turkish students per year between 1866 and 1907 was three, while the average number between 1908 and 1922 was 27, that is, eight times bigger than the previous period" (Sabev 2014: 164).

With regard to the Young Turks' Revolution, Caleb Gates stated: "The year 1908 was memorable for the rise of the Young Turks from whose ranks sprang the Committee of Union and Progress. This group of reformers was called Young Turks, not because of the age of its members but because of new ideals which they represented. The members of the party, some as exiles in foreign lands had laboured for years, in secret and in the press, to cultivate democratic principles and to resist the oppressive absolutism of the sultan. They aimed to establish a constitutional government… The committee of Union and Progress was eventually controlled by a triumvirate composed of Talat Pasha, Djemal Pasha and Enver Pasha" (Freely 2000: 171). According to Gates, Talat Pasha had always had a benevolent view of Robert College. With the Young Turks' revolution, the constitution of 1878 was reinstated with the intervention of the army that was working under the direction of the Committee of Union and Progress. The Committee continued to direct the affairs of the government after the assembling of Parliament. It constructed a large representation in the Parliament and controlled cabinet ministers. Until the revolution, Turks constituted 3–5 percent of Robert College, while in 1913 they were 15 percent (Sezer 1999, in Sabev 2014: 165). When the Sultanate came to an end and the Turkish Republic was established, the number of Turks who attended Robert College increased, following a decrease in the years 1920–1922, no doubt due to turmoil in the country caused by the War of Independence (Sabev 2014: 167).

As the number of Turkish students increased in the College, nationalism became one of the most significant topics and the religious character of the school was again questioned. In his memoir Gates states that: "Robert College and other American educational institutions in Turkey were established by Christian men and supported by their gifts. Their charters provided for instruction in the scriptures and for Christian worship, and required that their faculties should be composed of men of Christian character. For seventy years, from its founding, the college maintained a weekly teacher's prayer meeting, held in the home of the president, and this was the centre of spiritual inspiration. However, when Moslems began to come to us in increasing numbers, the religious problem took on a different aspect. At first all students were required to attend a chapel service, but later this was made optional for Moslems" (Freely 2000: 173).

The school sometimes drew negative reactions from local inhabitants as they were either verbally humiliated or stoned. Furthermore, the College was also criticised by some as it was considered to be making political propaganda rather than being an educational institution. George Washburn writes that one of the reasons why Turks were reluctant to send their children to Robert College was because it was built upon the Protestant faith. Interestingly, some Turks were afraid of the Protestant belief. It was believed that if the College excluded religious classes from its curriculum it would be very crowded with Turks (Sabev 2014: 164). It was also found that the political turmoil in the country influenced the number of Turkish students enrolled. For example, between 1880–1882 there were only 9–10 Turkish students in the College. Their number further dropped in the following years (Sabev 2014: 160). In the year of 1885–86, the Turkish authorities attempted to discourage the enrolment of Turkish students. In 1908, a Turkish Student Society was started in the College by Tevfik Fikret who was Professor of Turkish from late 1896 to 1915. Its objective was to improve the ability of students to debate and communicate as well as improving their analytical thinking (Sabev 2014: 163).

After the 1908 revolution, more high ranking officials decided to send their children to Robert College. These included some who even lived close to the college such as grand viziers Aali (Mehmed Emin Âli) Pasha (1867–1871), Mahmoud Nedim Pasha (1875), Mahomet Ruchdi (Mehmed Rüşdü) Pasha (1876). Many of them expressed their sympathy for the College and even "were much impressed by the experiments" done with the scientific apparatus that the college purchased in 1873 (Washburn 2013: 170). Moreover, at the time of the Second Constitutional Era, it was observed that the children of merchants and officers exceeded that of government officials. This was due to the fact that the number of Turkish/Muslim merchants increased after the Crimean War and the Ottoman-Russian War of 1877–78. The abolition of capitulations also contributed to an increase in Turkish students (Emin 1930, in Sabev 2014: 172). The number of students whose fathers were landowners increased from 8–17 percent and exceeded that of officials in central administration which decreased from 32 to 14 percent.

The academic year of 1912–1913 marked a huge challenge to the school in the form of the Balkan Wars. Caleb Gates wrote: "It can easily be imagined what a severe test was imposed upon the students of Robert College by these events. Their respective nations were at war with one another. Students and teachers were being called for military service, and many were anxious to know the fate of their families. The boys read the papers eagerly and all sorts of rumors were circulated." However, despite the war, students continued to sustain their friendships and Gates further adds: "While this war was raging, a boy from one Balkan country said to a fellow student from an enemy country: "If I were to meet you in the mountains of Macedonia it would be my duty to shoot you, but here we will live like brothers." Students frequently told each other that when they graduated they would do their best to prevent such wars. When a boy received tidings of the death of a relative, it was often a boy from an enemy country who was the first to console him" (Gates 1940: 203).

In the year of 1913–1914, Robert College completed fifty-one years of operation. The College owned about fifty acres of land, seven large school buildings, sixteen dwelling houses and a laundry. The faculty consisted of sixty five, the number of students was 550 and there were 635 graduates. In terms of the College's curriculum, it offered a classical course, a scientific course and engineering schools, together with instruction in commerce and music: both instrumental and vocal as detailed above. World War I brought about significant changes within the Ottoman Empire, however, Robert College was determined to open for the new academic year in 1914. Dr. Gates stated: "My colleagues had been discussing whether the College should open for the new school year. There was no doubt in my mind. The College always opened in September... in mid-September the College opened with an enrolment of four hundred and ten students" (Freely 2000: 210).

In 1915, Robert College had 27 graduates. Two among them received degrees in the Engineering School. There were 6 Armenians, 7 Bulgarians, 10 Greeks, 2 Turks and 2 other graduands. Furthermore, changes took place with regard to the College's curriculum. In 1915, the Ottoman government issued the "Regulation for Private Schools". It stipulated that "in the schools where the language of instruction is not Turkish there must be classes in the Turkish language, Turkish history and Turkish geography taught by Turkish teachers and each foreign school must appoint a co-director of Turkish origin who will control the school correspondence" (Sezer 1999: 41).

In the year of 1915–16, Gates writes: "The war had a dire effect upon living conditions in Turkey. Coal, charcoal and oil were at prices which staggered even the well-to-do. Sugar, rice, coffee, flour, matches and other staple supplies were sold at exorbitant rates. Many people around us were plunged into the deepest poverty. To relieve the distress, in our village of Rumeli Hisari, the Robert College community founded the Hisar Charitable Society which gave milk to children and food to families, provided work for widows and medicare for the sick, making no discrimination, of course, between Christians and Moslems" (Freely 2000: 215).

In February 1919, the first issue of a new monthly magazine called the Robert College Record was published. In the academic year of 1919–20, there were twenty different ethnic groups and 662 students. That year was also marked by an increase in the numbers of Albanian and Russian students enrolled. There were 257 Greeks, 179 Armenians, 103 Turks, 41 Israelites, 34 Bulgarians, 9 Albanians, 9 Russians, 5 Syrians, 5 Circassians, 4 Persians, 3 Americans, 3 Serbians, 2 English, 2 Swiss, 1 French, 1 Polish, 1 Chaldean, 1 Moroccan, 1 Rumanian, 1 Yugoslav. The overall student number could be further broken down into 379 enrolled in the Prepatory Department; 232 in the College; 51 in the Engineering School. In 1920, significant political changes took place in the Empire. It was the year when the National Grand Assembly was established and Mustafa Kemal was chosen as its president. In the same year, the Treaty of Sevres was signed which resulted in great loss of territory for the Ottoman Empire (Freely 2000).

In the year 1922–23, foreign ambassadors and ministers were not allowed to intervene on behalf of their national subjects in matters of education, and the administrators of educational establishments had to communicate with Turkish officials. During the peace negotiations at Lausanne, Ismet Pasha, who was the Commissioner for Foreign Affairs as well as the head of the Turkish Peace Delegation, gave assurances that his government would support the work of the American missionary schools. When the Treaty of Lausanne was signed on 24th July 1923, the Republic of Turkey's present boundaries were established, except for Hatay in the far south east which was acquired after a referendum in 1939. Furthermore, the Treaty included an agreement between Greece and Turkey for the exchange of their minorities, which meant approximately 1.3 million Greeks and 1 million Turks. With regard to the new Turkish Republic, Dr. Gates stated: "Turkey had been at a war for a decade. Utterly defeated in 1918, her people had risen almost miraculously to outwit the Allies, achieve national unity, and win a decisive victory over the Greeks, not as the pleading representative of the 'Sick Man of Europe'" (Freely 2000: 219).

In 1923–24 Robert College was put into the category of private schools under the supervision and control of the Turkish Department of Public Instruction. This department further asked for all the decrees of grant (firmans) given to the College by the former Sultans, in order that new equivalents could be issued by the Republic of Turkey. In that year there were 471 enrolments which was a decrease of more than 20 percent compared to the previous year. The enrolment of Armenians decreased by 102 and that of Greeks by 82. However, the number of Turks enrolling increased by 49 (Washburn 2013).

Conclusion

In conclusion, the American missionary undertaking started to take root in the world following the creation of the American Board of Commissioners for Foreign Missions. American missionaries first aimed at evangelizing Native Americans in the Americas, but they soon broadened their mission by establishing missionary stations in different corners of the world. One of the most strategic missionary settlements was Jerusalem which was then part of the Ottoman Empire. Before American missionaries reached the Ottoman Empire, there had been little Ottoman-American diplomacy, with the first American-Ottoman encounters dating back to the late eighteenth century. With the arrival of American missionaries in the Empire, their representation and protection became a significant issue which eventually led to the commencement of formal diplomatic relations. With regard to the Ottoman Empire's political climate at this time, it was losing its power due to wars and invasions. In order to protect its integrity, the empire sought to modernize its political, social and military system by adopting western measures and granting liberties to minorities. After the imperial decrees of 1839 and 1856, American missionaries increased their activities and started to be recognized by the Empire. Ottoman Empire officials further considered that the Empire could best be transformed via education. This book argues that American missionary schools were one of the most significant vehicles that spread western ideals in the Empire and became models for the Turkish education system. The book further suggests that Robert College can be considered as one of the most successful examples of such enterprise, which to this day still preserves its high ranking prestige. Over a comparatively short period of time, the College grew to become one of the most significant schools in the Ottoman Empire, and when the Empire collapsed it became not only one of the most distinguished schools in Turkey, but also in the Middle East and Balkans. In the Ottoman period, it would seem that the College owed its distinguished position in comparison to other missionary schools and colleges, to its secular education and its equitable policies with regard to different ethnic and religious groups. In the case of Republican Turkey, its continued success can be ascribed to the College distancing itself from political matters and not trying to interfere with the institutions of Turkey. The College, as recorded earlier in this work, only focused on education and made a tremendous effort to raise the school to world standards (Rosenbloom 1969, Hamlin 2014, Pamuk 2016).

Robert College also benefited from three strong leaders over the first 69 years of its existence. Cyrus Hamlin who established the College was in charge from 1863–77. He was followed by George Washburn who led the College from 1877–1903. Finally, Caleb Gates who not only held the role of College President for a record 29 years from 1903–32, but also handled the difficult task of steering the College through World War I, followed by the transition from the Ottoman Empire to the newly formed Republic of Turkey. All three no doubt gained strength and stamina in their work from their Protestant faith. Yet they also had the wisdom to understand that faith is an individual choice, and a humanistic approach to education would seem to produce the best results.

Not only did the College benefit from these three outstanding leaders, it also aimed at hiring the best and most devoted teachers capable of delivering its broad, intensive curriculum. In the Ottoman period students in the College studied a variety of subjects for long hours including no less than four languages. The Turkish Republic adopted a new education system which led to a shortening of course hours, the reduction from four to two languages, some subjects being taught in Turkish by Turkish teachers, and a new complementary approach between subjects.

Finally, in terms of forging strong diplomatic relations between the USA and Turkey, in August 1999 there was a devastating earthquake in western Turkey which killed many thousands of people and caused major structural damage. In November that year President Clinton visited Turkey and made a speech to the Turkish parliament in which he said: "I have come to express America's solidarity with the Turkish people at a time of national tragedy, and to reaffirm our partnership for a common future. We have been friends for a very long time. In 1863, the first American college outside the United States, Robert College, opened its doors to the youth of Turkey...........I'm very proud that Prime Minister Ecevit is an alumnus of Robert College" (Clinton 1999).

Bibliography

ABCFM, Annual Report 1823

ABCFM, Annual Report 1834

ABCFM, Annual Report 1845

ABCFM, Annual Report 1856

Acun, Fatma and Gürtunca, Evrim Şencan. 2016. "Osmanlı'dan Cumhuriyet'e Robert Kolej'de Eğitim." *Tarih İncelemeleri Dergisi* 31(1): 1–34. http://dergipark.gov.tr/egetid/issue/23836/253933.

Akgün, Secil. 1989. "The Turkish Image in the Reports of American Missionaries in the Ottoman Empire." *Turkish Studies Association Bulletin.* 13(94): 91–105. http://www.jstor.org/stable/43385311.

Anderson, Rufus. 1872. *History of the Missions of the American Board of Commissioners for Foreign Missions to the Oriental Churches.* Boston: ABCFM.

Aydın, Mehmet. 2005. *Türkiye'de Misyonerlik Faaliyetleri.* Ankara: Türkiye Diyanet Vakfı Yayınları.

Barlett, Samuel Colcord. 2015. *Historical Sketch of the Missions of the American Board in Turkey.* Australia: Leopold Classic Library.

Baytop, Turhan. 2003. *Antep'in Öncü Hekimleri Merkezi Türkiye Koleji Tıp Bölümü ve Antep Amerikan Hastanesi.* Istanbul: SEV Yayınları.

Bozkurt, Gülnihal. 1989. *Gayri Müslim Osmanlı Vatandaşlarının Hukuki Durumu.* Ankara: TTK Basımevi.

Cilacı, Osman. 1982. *Hıristiyanlık Propagandası ve Misyoner Faaliyetleri.* Ankara: Diyanet Vakfı Yayınları.

Clinton, William J. 1999. "Remarks to the Turkish Grand National Assembly in Ankara." *The American Presidency Project* (Nov 15, 1999), http://www.presidency.ucsb.edu/ws/?pid=56935. (accessed 10 May 2016)

Danacıoglu, Esra. 1993. "Osmanlı Anadolu'sunda Anglo-Sakson (Protestan) Misyoner Faaliyetleri (1816–1856)." PhD dissertation, Dokuz Eylül University.

Devrim, Ümit. 2014. "The American Protestant Missionary Network in Ottoman Turkey, 1876–1914." *International Journal of Humanities and*

Social Science Vol 4, no 6(1): 16–51. http://www.ijhssnet.com/journals/ Vol_4_No_6_1_April_2014/3.pdf.

Dodge, Bayard. 1972. "American Educational and Missionary Efforts in the Nineteenth and Early Twentieth Centuries." *The Annals of the American Academy of Political and Social Science 401*. http://www.jstor.org/ stable/1039108.

Dogan, Mehmet Ali. 2013. "American Board of Commissioners for Foreign Missions (ABCFM) and "Nominal Christians": Elias Riggs (1810–1901) and American Missionary Activities in the Ottoman Empire." PhD dissertation, the University of Utah.

Erhan, Cagri. 2000. "Ottoman official attitudes towards American missionaries." *Milletlerarası Münasebetler Türk Yıllığı-The Turkish Yearbook of International Relation*, 315–341. http://intcommunity.org/wp-content/ uploads/2018/02/Ottoman_Official_Attitudes-Cagri_Erhan.pdf.

Field, James, A. 1969. *America and the Mediterranean World, 1776–1882*. Princeton: Princeton University Press.

Finnie, David H. (1967). *Pioneers East: The Early American Experience in the Middle East*. Cambridge: Harvard University Press.

Freely, John. 2000. *A History of Robert College: the American College for Girls, and Boğaziçi University*. Istanbul: Yapi Kredi Yayinlari.

Gates, Caleb. F. 1940. *Not to Me Only*. Princeton: Princeton University Press.

Gordon, Leland G. 1932. *American Relations with Turkey, 1830–1930*. Philadelphia: University of Pennsylvania Press.

Grabill, Joseph. L. 1971. *Protestant Diplomacy and the Near East: Missionary Influence on American Policy 1810–1927*. Minneapolis: University of Minnesota Press.

Greenwood, Keith. 2000. *Robert College: The American Founders*. Istanbul: Bogazici Üniversitesi Yayinevi.

Hamlin, Cyrus. 1889. "Robert College, Constantinople" *American Antiquarian Society*. https://www.americanantiquarian.org/proceedings/ 48057586.pdf.

Hamlin, Cyrus. 1893. *My Life and Times*. Chicago: The Pilgrim Press.

Hamlin, Cyrus. 2014. *Among The Turks*. Istanbul: Bogazici Universitesi Yayinevi.

Harlow, Samuel Ralph. 1919. *Student Witnesses for Christ*. New York: Association Press.

Kennedy, Judd W. 2008. "American Missionaries in Turkey and Northern Syria and the Development of Central Turkey *and* Aleppo Colleges, 1874–1967." Undergraduate Thesis, College of William & Mary.

Kerner, Howard Joseph. 1948. "Turco-American Diplomatic Relations 1860–1880." Ph.D Thesis, Georgetown University.

Kirsehirlioglu, Erol. 1963. *Türkiye'de Misyoner Faaliyetleri*. Istanbul: Bedir Yayınevi.

Kışlalı, Ahmet Taner. 2003. *Siyasal Sistemler Siyasal Çatışma ve Uzlaşma*. Ankara: Imge Kitabevi.

Kocabasoglu, Uygur. 1988. *Osmanlı Imparatorlugunda XIX. Yuzyilda Amerikan Yuksek Okullari*. Ankara: Mulkiyeliler Birligi Vakfı.

Kocabasoglu, Uygur. 2000. *Anadolu'daki Amerika*. Ankara: İmge Kitabevi.

Marriott, Sir John A. R. 1966. *The Eastern Question: An Historical Study in European Diplomacy*. Oxford: Oxford University Press.

Neill, Stephen. 1986. *A History of Christian Missions*. London: Penguin Books.

Ortaylı, Ilber. 1981. "Osmanlı İmparatorlugunda Amerikan Okulları Üzerine Bazı Gözlemler" *Amme İdaresi Dergisi* 14 no. 13.

Pamuk, Orhan. 2016. *Istanbul*. Istanbul: Yapı Kredi Yayınları.

Polvan, Nurettin. 1952. *Türkiye'de Yabancı Öğretim*. Istanbul: Milli Egitim Bakanlığı Yayınları.

Porter, David. 1875. *Memoir of Commodore David Porter*. Albany, NY: J. Munsell.

Prime, Edward Dorr Griffin. 1876. *Forty years in the Turkish empire, Memoirs of Rev. William Goodell, D.D., late missionary of the A.B.C.F.M. at Constantinople*. New York: Robert Carter and Brothers.

Rosenbloom, Joseph R. 1969. "A Profile of Robert College Graduates." *The Muslim World* 59(2): 153–157. https://doi.org/10.1111/j.1478-1913.1969.tb00482.x.

Sabev, Orlin. 2011. "A Tower of Babel in Constantinople: Robert College's Students and Their Nationality." *Études balkaniques* 47(23): 117–159.

Sabev, Orlin. 2014. "The Muslim/Turkish Students of Robert College (1866–1925)." *Osmanlı İstanbulu I. Uluslararası Osmanlı İstanbulu*

Sempozyumu Bildirileri. İstanbul: İstanbul Büyükşehir Belediyesi, 141–95. https://osmanliistanbulu.org/tr/images/osmanliistanbulu-1/11_orlin-sabev. pdf.

Sahin, Emrah. 2004. "Errand in the East. A History of Evangelical American Protestant Missionaries and Their Missions to Ottoman Istanbul during the Nineteenth Century." Master's Thesis, Bilkent University.

Salt, Jeremy. 2002. "Trouble Wherever They Went: American Missionaries in Anatolia and Ottoman Syria in the Nineteenth Century." *The Muslim World* 92: 287–313. doi: 10.1111/j.1478–1913.2002.tb03745.x.

Sezer, Ayten. 1999. *Atatürk Döneminde Yabancı Okulları (1923–1938).* Ankara: Türk Tarih Kurumu Yayınevi.

Shelton, Elizabeth W. 2011. "Faith, Freedom, and Flag: The Influence of American Missionaries in Turkey on Foreign Affairs, 1830–1880." PhD dissertation, Georgetown University.

Şişman, Adnan. 2002. *Misyonerlik ve Osmanlı Devleti'nin Son Döneminde Kurulan Yabancı Sosyal ve Kültürel Müesseseler.* Ankara: Yeni Türkiye Yayınları.

Stone, Frank A. 2006. *Academies for Anatolia: A Study of the Rationale, Program, and Impact of the Educational Institutions Sponsored by the American Board in Turkey.* San Francisco, CA: Caddo Gap Press.

Strong, William E. 1910. *The Story of the American Board: An Account of the First Hundred Years of the American Board of Commissioners for Foreign Missions.* Boston: Pilgrim Press.

Taskin, Faruk. 2007. "Amerikan Misyoner Okullarindan "Merkezi Türkiye Koleji" (1876–1924)." Master's Thesis, Mersin University.

Temple, Daniel H. 1855. *Life and Letters of Rev. Daniel Temple, for Twenty Years a Missionary of the A.B.C.F.M. in Western Asia.* Boston: Congregational Board of Publication.

The Missionary Herald 21, 1825

The Missionary Herald 26, 6 June 1830

The Missionary Herald 30, no. 11, Nov. 1834

The Missionary Herald Vol. 93 No. 10 Oct 1897

The Missionary Herald: Reports from Ottoman Syria. 1819–1870

Turan, Ömer. 1999. "Osmanlı'dan Cumhuriyet'e Türkiye'de Protestan Misyonerlik Faaliyetleri." *Osmanli*. Ankara: Yeni Türkiye Yayınları. 204–211.

Vahapoglu, Hidayet. 2005. *Osmanlıdan Günümüze Azınlık ve Yabancı Okullari*. Istanbul: M.E.B. Yayınları.

Washburn, George. 2013. *Fifty Years in Constantinople: and Recollections of Robert College*. Istanbul: Bogazici University Press.

Washburn, George. 1909. *Fifty Years in Constantinople and Recollections of Robert College*. Boston and New York: Houghton Mifflin.

Weber, Max. 1997. *Protestan Ahlakı ve Kapitalizmin Ruhu* (trans. Zeynep Gürata). Ankara: Ayraç Yayınevi.

Yücel, Idris. 2012. "A Missionary Society at the Crossroads: American Missionaries on the eve of the Turkish Republic." *Cumhuriyet Tarihi Araştırmaları Dergisi* 8 (15): 51–65. http://www.ctad.hacettepe.edu.tr/8_15/4.pdf).